The Emotional Eating Rescue Plan
for Smart, Busy Women

The Emotional Eating Rescue Plan

for Smart, Busy Women

Make Peace with Food, Live the Life You Hunger For

Melissa McCreery, PhD

ISBN-10: 0989373703
ISBN-13: 978-0-9893737-0-8
Library of Congress Control Number: 2013907984

Book Cover and Book Design: Ryan Scheife at Mayfly Design
Editor: Lorraine E. Fisher at Off Ramp Publishing

Cover photographs courtesy of iStockphoto: GlobalStock (Lifebuoy); krystiannawrocki (Blue Water Surface); Turnervisual (Choc Chip Cookie); JC559 (pretzel); pepifoto (Potato chips); eyewave (chocolate covered donut)

Published in the United States of America

Note: Information from this book should not be used as a substitute for professional medical or psychological care or attention, nor should it be inferred as such. This publication is intended to provide helpful and informative material on the subject matter covered. It is sold with the understanding that the author and publisher are not engaged in rendering professional services in the book. If the reader requires personal assistance or advice, a competent professional should be consulted. Always check with your medical or mental health professional if you have questions or concerns about a specific condition and be sure to check with your health-care provider before making any changes to your diet. The author and the publisher specifically disclaim any responsibility for any liability, loss, or risk, personal or otherwise, which is incurred as a consequence, directly or indirectly, of the use and application of any of the contents of this book.

Published by Too Much on Her Plate, Bellingham, WA
info@toomuchonherplate.com

Contents

Introduction .... *vii*

Creating Real Change 1

The Emotional Eating Rescue Plan for Smart, Busy Women:
Your New Tools

Week One: Curiosity 21

Week Two: Meeting Your Needs
without Turning to Food 47

Week Three: Ingredients for Success 101

Week Four: Setting Your GPS 125

What Comes After the Rescue? *157*

Rescue Plan Resource Lists *161*

Acknowledgements *165*

About the Author *163*

Introduction

Welcome to *The Emotional Eating Rescue Plan for Smart, Busy Women*. I want to thank you for investing your time, your energy and your hope in this program. I know changing engrained habits can be a challenge, and I have a great deal of respect for what it takes to try something new—especially if you've tried before to make changes with your eating and your weight and you feel like you've failed. There are countless people nursing far too many broken dreams around weight loss and overeating.

People often ask me why I wrote this book and why I do the work that I do. Yes, I'm a clinical psychologist and an emotional eating expert, and I've worked in this field for more than 20 years. But, like almost *all* women, I also have a story with food, weight and overeating, and if I was you, I'd be wondering what that story was and how that's impacted the rescue plan I'm sharing with you here.

So here's what I can tell you.

When people ask me what my own story is with overeating and weight gain, I often feel like a fraud.

I feel like a fraud because these struggles are so *not* a part of my life or of who I am today. To talk about what I went through in the past almost feels unbelievable to me now.

Almost. It's a description of another place and time and so far removed from where I am now, from how I eat, from how I feel and think about and relate to food, that it almost feels strange to talk about it. My battles with overeating and weight no longer define me. In fact, they no longer exist.

But they did.

I had years when struggles with food and weight and how to eat took up far more energy than I can now quite believe. I've binged, grazed, starved and visited the scale compulsively. I've skipped meals and tried to live on crazy diets and food plans until I had no idea whether I was hungry or full or what I should be eating. My weight was a moving target, but any weight loss I achieved never lasted, and the final result always seemed to be five more pounds than when I had started. There was a time when I had four different sizes of pants in my closet, and I needed them all to be sure I'd have something to wear. There were "good days" and "bad days" depending on how I ate, and bad days always ended in more eating. Despite what I accomplished in other areas of my life, the feeling that I couldn't control my eating or my weight haunted me and left me feeling ineffective and stupid for struggling with something that seemed like it should be so straightforward and effortless.

My struggles with food meshed perfectly with my high-achieving spirit and a constant nagging belief that I needed to *do more*, that there was always more to accomplish and more to prove. Perfectionism, wanting to please, and the often unrealistic expectations I had for myself contributed to using food to fill voids, provide comfort, numb my emotions and manage stress.

Thankfully, I found a way out. It took a while and included many false starts, but with lots of persistence, I found the combination of the right help and strategies that let me step sideways and exit the crazy emotional eating roller coaster on which I had been trapped. This wasn't a temporary fix (been there, tried that unsatisfying route). Instead, I found a way to create a permanent, solid ease and peace with food, with eating and with my weight. I left the crazy overeating madness behind, and I never looked back. Or I never meant to.

Fate had different plans for me. Despite my loudly stated intentions, my career path as a clinical psychologist and later as a coach, consultant and speaker, seemed continually to veer toward women's struggles with food and weight from the very beginning. I now see that what compelled me to work in this arena was knowing how deep the suffering is with overeating and weight battles, how powerless it can make us feel, and the profound healing and transformation that is absolutely possible—but that few people talk about. My personal experiences led to my interest which led to lots of learning and research and thousands of hours of clinical work with women who were *beyond* sick and tired of struggling with overeating, emotional eating and weight.

I believe we deserve to be living the best version of our lives, yet over the years, I've repeatedly witnessed the way struggles with emotional eating are robbing women of their sense of effectiveness and their confidence in their ability to be successful. I work with busy, high-achieving women all over the world who have had great success in many areas of their lives—they are wonderful mothers, successful business owners, leaders in their professions—amazingly talented women who seemingly can do *anything*—and yet they are so frustrated with themselves because they can't figure out why they haven't been successful with eating less and losing weight.

In many ways, overeating and emotional eating can become side effects of the high-achieving, busy lifestyles many of us are living. Food is an all-too-convenient way to comfort, soothe and reward ourselves when we don't feel like we have time to do anything else. It's always available, we can partake fairly mindlessly, and we usually don't have to say no to anyone or anything in order to treat ourselves.

Smart busy women already know that when they are overeating they need to eat less and that emotional eating isn't helping them. The problem is, it's not what you know, it's what you can *do*, and when you have a lot on your plate—both figuratively and literally—you probably don't need more rules, more "shoulds," and more on your to-do list—you need a whole new approach to food that addresses why it's so darn powerful in your life to begin with.

And *this* is what *The Emotional Eating Rescue Plan for Smart, Busy Women* is all about.

The tools, steps and strategies in the rescue plan have changed my life and those of many of my clients forever.

Today—in fact, it's been for decades now—I eat with ease. I eat for taste and pleasure *and* for fuel. My weight is relatively stable, and if I notice a change, I know what to do. I don't weigh myself (I don't even think about it), and the pants in my closet are all one size.

Since making peace with food, I've had challenges as we all do. I invite more stress than I would like. I've had two healthy pregnancies where I gained and lost close to 60 pounds each time. I had a frustrating and confusing battle with undiagnosed hypothyroidism that completely threw my metabolism out of whack, and as I am now in my late forties, my hormones are having fun with me again. I'm busy and I juggle a lot. That's life, right?

It's not always a piece of cake, but when it comes to food, eating and weight, *the struggle is gone*, and I'm the one in the driver's seat. The tools and the strategies in this rescue plan work. I'm living them. In fact, they've allowed me to have my life.

I've been sharing this approach with the clients in my coaching and consulting practice and programs, and they've encouraged me to share it with you. My hope is that my journey and the path of the rescue plan will assist you and bring more ease and peace to *your* life.

I'm here to help you.

Take good care,
Melissa

Creating Real Change

(Not the lame and unsatisfying diet roller coaster stuff)

Diets *don't* work. You already know this (at least one part of your brain probably does).You're a smart woman, and you've probably been around the block more than a few times with weight loss, willpower and the whole vicious cycle. The research is clear. Most people who lose weight on a diet will gain it back. In fact, some experts estimate that more than 80 percent of people who have lost weight regain all of it, or more, after two years. One systematic analysis of 31 long-term diet studies revealed that about two-thirds of dieters regained *more* weight within four or five years than they initially lost[1]. Diets don't work, and still, bookstores are filled with books carefully enumerating *the* recipe for weight loss.

If it were really as simple as identifying the perfect food formula, don't you think the diet book writers would have figured it out by now? Oprah would have reached her dream weight, and we wouldn't be sharing these words.

The sad truth is that most of the diet books and weight loss gurus miss the point entirely. Trying to solve overeating problems by focusing on food doesn't get you anywhere.

---

1   Mann, T., Tomiyama, A. J., Westling, E., Lew, A., Samuels, B., & Chatman, J. (2007). Medicare's search for effective obesity treatments: Diets are not the answer. American Psychologist, 62, 220-233.

Because much of the time, it's not about *what* you eat, it's about *why*. And it's about knowing what you can do *instead* of going through the drive thru, nibbling at the leftover brownies, or demolishing the whole bag of chips.

A diet may sound like the logical solution to overeating, but in most cases it will lead you off track. Think about it: most dieters don't achieve their dream weight, and they don't end up feeling comfortable and at ease with their eating. Instead, over time, they become experts at weight loss—and at dieting. Many of the women who seek my help know more than they ever wanted to about nutrition and weight loss. They could literally write books about what they believe they "should" be doing.

But what they know isn't helping. Knowing what to do isn't enough when something powerful is keeping overeaters from being able to do what they think they should—eat less. Something extraordinarily compelling keeps millions of smart, talented women overeating despite the fact that they are trying not to. And every year it leads to endless hours of frustration and countless dollars wasted on weight loss "solutions."

Still, the idea of a diet, a simple plan that can create magical results, is appealing, and dieters do lose a lot of weight—over and over again. While this keeps the diet industry in business, it doesn't create real (lasting) results or lead to a pant size you can count on.

There is a much bigger, brighter and shinier goal than weight loss that I'm going to encourage you to study and eventually adopt as your own. The goal I'm referring to is one of creating ease and *peace with food*, learning to feed yourself what you are *really* hungry for, and by doing this, relaxing into a way of eating, and by extension, a weight that feels good on you.

That's what *The Emotional Eating Rescue Plan for Smart, Busy Women* is all about. This is not a diet program. You won't find formulas here for calculating your daily intake or talk of carbohydrates and fat grams. In fact, this plan turns much of the way you think about weight loss upside down. It's not a program about deprivation; it's a system about *transformation* and about feeding yourself. This action plan will show you—step by step—how to develop your own personalized plan for feeding yourself the way YOU need to be fed.

The Emotional Eating Rescue Plan for Smart, Busy Women is a step-by-step four week program that will teach you the tools you need to address emotional eating and overeating challenges and help you integrate the tools into your busy life in a way that works for you.

The action steps I'm going to share will help you re-learn how to put food in a better place in your life—one that feels easier and less filled with struggle. I'm going to walk you through smart, simple steps to help you stop obsessing about food and to stop being mired in guilt about what you eat.

You won't go hungry if you follow the plan here; in fact, you'll probably end up feeling less hungry than you have in a long time. The information, plan and action steps will help you change your relationship with food at the same time you are learning powerful new tools that will help you make these changes permanent.

The goal of the Emotional Eating Rescue Plan is to help you create *lasting changes* that will let you stop obsessing about food, move beyond dieting and get on with your life. When you start taking these steps—and feeding your-self what you *really* crave—you'll likely notice positive changes that extend far beyond your eating and that start transforming your life. Pretty cool!

There is a lot of important information in the rescue plan—some within the pages and some within yourself—that you will glean from reading and following the steps in this book. I strongly encourage you to try *all* the activities and attempt to answer all the questions. *Pay particular attention* if there are some exercises you are certain you don't want to do. Be curious about that, and I suggest that you try them anyway.

Oftentimes the places with the most potential learning are the places about which we are most protective or where we feel most resistant.

We can all benefit from extra help and guidance from time to time (sometimes, a lot more than we tend to allow ourselves to seek). Throughout this book I'll point out additional resources or places where you can delve more deeply into a particular topic. You'll also find a comprehensive list of all these resources at the end of the book.

As you dive into the Emotional Eating Rescue Plan, be gentle with yourself but be persistent. Remember, the end result of this program is more peace and ease and absolutely NOT having to go hungry anymore.

Food for Thought

Bear with me for a little more diet talk, and then, I promise we'll leave the old ways behind.

If I told you that most people will lose weight by eating only two cans of tuna, three apples and eight glasses of water every day, it would be true. If I wrote a book, or posted online about the wonders of this diet, certain folks would try it and would probably lose weight (please don't try it—I just made it up this second). As with most diets, however, the weight loss effects of this one would probably wear off rather quickly, and the book would end up on a table at the next garage sale.

I'm sure this sounds eerily familiar. You may have been to this rodeo before (or tried a diet that was just as rigid or daunting). It's a rare individual who is willing to consume only two cans of tuna, three apples and eight glasses of water every single day. It's an even rarer individual who would find it pleasant and who would want to continue doing it. The diet itself is not nutritionally balanced, and our bodies, because they require a broader balance of nutrients and more calories, would be working against us on this plan, making it physically hard to sustain both the nutritional monotony and the weight loss. After a while (probably not too long), we wouldn't feel so good and we wouldn't function very well—decreasing our ability to stick with "the plan." In short, our bodies, our minds and our senses would start screaming in rebellion.

Regardless of whether this tuna-apple plan causes weight loss, few would follow it. Those who follow it aren't likely to stay on it. And even those who stay on it and lose the weight they want—what are they supposed to do then? The plan makes no provision at all for how to sustain the weight loss they've achieved or how to feed their bodies for the rest of their lives—bodies which, by the time they've stopped the "diet" are so sensory-deprived, nutritionally limited, calorically-depleted, and just plain tired of being treated this way, that they're poised for rebellion and weight re-gain.

The above scenario describes in a nutshell why diets don't work. It may be an extreme example, in order to make the point, but after examining a variety of diets, you'll find it's actually not that far off base.

Why Do We Eat, and What Does that Have to Do With Eskimos and Snow?

Few people in our culture use food strictly as fuel. We eat for taste. We eat for entertainment. We eat because we are bored, tired, excited or heartbroken. Many of us eat *big time* when we are stressed. We eat as part of a social experience. We eat because advertisers spend millions of dollars enticing us in a variety of ways and equating foods with happiness, sex, excitement, even riches and fame.

What are you really hungry *for*?

Let's look at the concept of hunger for a moment. The dictionary on my bookshelf (American Heritage) defines hunger as *a strong desire for food*. Notice that this is a broader definition than "a physiological need for food." Here, hunger is defined as *wanting food very badly*, which is different from *needing food to survive*. The definition focuses on the *desire* for the food. It doesn't address *why* the food is desired.

If I skip down a few lines to the third definition of hunger, I find: *a strong desire or craving*. Hunger can be experienced for something that is not food. I can hunger for attention or companionship or control. I can be hungry for lots of things. And that is the ticket. Hunger does not have to be about food, and even when it *is* a hunger for food, it may signal that we want it for reasons other than physical need. At these times we can feed ourselves in ways other than eating. If we know how.

Let me say that again because it is important.

We experience hunger in many areas of our life. We hunger in relationships, we hunger to have our emotional needs met. We hunger for physical energy or for sensory pleasure. Hunger is pervasive in our lives, yet it is not always about food, NOR is a craving or hunger for food always a physical need for nourishment.

You've probably heard that Eskimos have a broad vocabulary for talking about snow. The languages of Alaskan Native Peoples are rich with a variety of words that describe various types of snow. This is because snow plays such a crucial part in their daily lives, and the ability to be precise about *which particular kind or type of snow* they are talking about is really important—much more important to their culture than it is for people living farther south.

Consider this in the context of hunger. As I've just been describing, hunger is an exceptionally rich phenomenon that can be experienced in many different ways and requires vastly different types of feeding, depending on which kind of hunger it is. If I'm hungry for love, I'm not really going to feel better if I feed myself chocolate chip ice cream—well, not for long anyway.

How precise is your language for identifying the different reasons that you eat? Do you have a word for eating when you are physically depleted and would eat anything offered to you? When you are eating because you are tired? Because the cake smells good? When you're out with friends and ordering the nachos is a tradition? What about the eating that is triggered by sadness or by a feeling of "I've worked hard all day and I deserve this?" Is there a word for the "zoned-out" eating that happens when you're watching TV and before you realize it, the bag of chips is half gone?

Most people describe all these hungers in pretty much the same way. Yet, the only thing they really have in common is the food that was used to feed the hunger. We don't have words for all these types of hunger—and that is both a problem and a symptom.

It's a problem because it limits our ability to be precise in what we are doing and why. When we are limited in our precision to understand ourselves—our hunger or anything else—we are limited in the choices we have about how to respond. If all we know is that we are "hungry" and hunger equals a need to eat, then the equation is simple.

The problem is that the equation is *wrong*.

In most of those examples, hunger did not equal a need for food. But when we respond to our hunger this way, we end up feeding ourselves poorly and being unable to meet our own needs. Remember, "feeding" refers to what you are doing to satisfy the need or craving. If you are feeding a need for love with ice cream, you are not really feeding yourself what you need. On top of this, when we respond too broadly to hunger with food, we end up eating food that our bodies don't need, possibly feeling physically uncomfortable and maybe even guilty and ashamed and out of control afterwards.

Our lack of precise vocabulary for describing our hungers is also a symptom of our culture. We live in a fast-paced world where we are encouraged, through lots of slick marketing efforts, to keep moving, to continue keeping up with everybody else, and to look to products and things to fulfill our needs. Food is sold to us—seldom as fuel—but as a great time with friends, an energy booster, the thing that will create a happy family moment. The emphasis is on the quick fix.

Far too few of us receive daily reminders and messages to slow down, to listen to ourselves, to take the time to figure out what we are hungry for and how to feed ourselves; to question whether the candy bar or the new pair of jeans will really feed the hungry spot inside us. Most of the time, it probably won't. If we're going to care, in a genuine and healthy way, for our hungers, we need to learn (or remember) how to care for *ourselves* in ways that are much more satisfying than food.

The Hunger is Real

The hungers that I'm talking about are *very real and extraordinarily powerful*. In fact, if we could hook ourselves up to some kind of monitor and measure all of our various hungers, we'd probably find that for most overeaters living in our culture, physical hunger isn't the dominant hunger by which they are plagued.

The Vicious Cycle—why diets don't work, weight gets regained, and people get stuck on a weight loss roller coaster

We're hungry—in many different ways and for many different things. That's a part of the human condition and there is nothing wrong with that. In fact, it's perfectly normal. Some people, for a variety of reasons, get out of touch with their hungers. Perhaps their hunger or appetites feel too overwhelming or feel impossible to feed. Maybe the hunger has been there for so long that it seemed like the best response was to try to "stop thinking about it." It might even feel like the hunger is so big that if we really let ourselves feel it, it will just swallow us up—or it will be unbearably big and painful and never go away.

Sometimes we haven't been taught *how* to pay attention to our hungers. We might experience them as just a vague sense that something is wrong. We might not really know what the hunger is or what to do about it.

If we were raised by people who were uncomfortable with their own hungers and with their own appetites (appetites for love, for indulgence, for stress-relief, for excitement and passion), we may have been taught to try to push our hungers aside or ignore them as our parents did. Or, we may have been taught indirect or inappropriate ways of responding to what we truly hunger for.

Many women have learned to experience their emotional and sensual hungers as a hunger for food. In fact, when they feel any—or many—of their hungers, they address them as if they were a need for food. Over time, the distinctions get blurred. The underlying real hunger might not even be consciously experienced. You have a vague (or intense) feeling of discomfort, and your brain tells you that you need to eat something. It can become almost as automatic as breathing—an impulse followed by an automatic response. The problem, of course, is that the original, real hunger never gets addressed. That hunger never gets fed. We might feel better for the moment, but the hunger will return.

The problem with diets (well, one of the problems with diets) is that they address our need to be fed on only one level—the level of our physical hunger. If you are eating to address a variety of hungers and someone cuts back your food supply, guess what? You are going to feel extremely hungry—in more ways than one. You may start to feel anxious and panicky. If food is something you are accustomed to using to feed yourself and your feelings, then when you cut back on the food, you are going to feel both very deprived, and very un-fed, *in multiple areas of your life.*

If you are able to maintain the diet for a while, you may start to see some weight loss. Meanwhile, all your unfed appetites continue to grow. Deprivation is not something that can be sustained permanently. Eventually, one or more of those hungers will become so big and unbearable that you will feed it in the only way you know how. If you have learned to feel your emotional hunger as a hunger for food, you'll eat. You might over-eat. You might even binge.

Remember: that hunger has been building without being fed. You are going to feel ravenous and sorely deprived. The problem is, it's not about the food. Food isn't what you need (assuming you've been getting adequate calories on this diet you've been on), and food isn't going to quench that hunger. At least not permanently.

As long as you remain within the diet paradigm, which keeps people focused on the issues of food and physiological hunger, you will miss the bigger and much more powerful picture. It's like focusing on one tree when the issue is really about the whole forest. *The Emotional Eating Rescue Plan for Smart, Busy Women* is going to help you tend the forest.

It's true that to lose weight, you need to eat less. But, you do not need to *feed* yourself less, and you do not need to go hungry. This book will give you the steps to becoming an expert on your hungers and to learning to match your various hungry feelings accurately to the best way of feeding them. As you do this, you will be amazed to discover what a smaller place food naturally starts to take in your life. Because it's not about the food. It's about realizing that you *are* hungry *but* you've been feeding yourself in unsatisfying ways. When you know what you really, truly hunger for, it gets much easier to feed yourself in a way that will not only satisfy you, it will not contribute to your pant size.

Curiosity, *not* Judgment

> *"I think, at a child's birth, if a mother could ask a fairy godmother to endow it with the most useful gift, that gift would be curiosity."*
>
> —ELEANOR ROOSEVELT

If you've been living in the world of diets for a while, you are probably also immersed in the idea of deprivation. Dieters' heads are often filled with ideas about what they "should" be doing and guilt for not having done it. Dieters have lists of "good" and "bad" foods and live a life of "good" and "bad" days. The feeling of "shouldn't eat" or "shouldn't eat *that*" is pervasive.

I'm going to challenge you to step out of the culture of deprivation and into the process of *transformation*. This book is about truly feeding yourself—and savoring being fed. It's about finding ways to satisfy your appetites directly and in the best possible ways so that you feel good and so that your whole life benefits from the changes you've made.

The Emotional Eating Rescue Plan for Smart, Busy Women is not about guilt and being "good" or "bad." Making this major shift away from "good and bad thinking" and deprivation as a model for eating is a process that will occur over time. It certainly won't happen overnight.

The steps in this book will lead you through the process of learning new things about yourself, your appetites and the way that you feed and nurture yourself. It's designed to be a process with trials and errors and missteps and successes.

It's not a diet and you can't *blow it*.

Just keep taking one step at a time through the rescue plan and, I promise, it will all start to make sense in a powerful way.

I'll encourage you throughout this program to be *curious and not judgmental*.

The ability to be a curious observer about yourself is one of the most powerful skills you can hone. Curiosity (with a side of compassion) is the necessary skill for examining your life and your behavior, determining what is working well, what could be better, where you tend to get stuck and what gets in your way, and what kind of changes might help things go more smoothly in the future.

Curiosity is a completely different animal than criticism or judgment. Here's an example. Let's say there is a half a cheesecake in your refrigerator. You come home from work and by the time you are ready to go to bed, the cheesecake is mostly gone. You were home alone. Here's what happens when the judgmental voice in your head takes over:

You idiot, look what you've done. Now you've ruined a great day of dieting—you were doing so well and now you blew it. You always do this. I knew you couldn't have just one bite. Now you're going to be fatter than ever. Tomorrow you'll have to start all over again. You'll be so bloated. You are such a pig. Might as well finish these crumbs. I knew you couldn't cope with having sweets in the house. I'll have to throw everything out and start fresh tomorrow. Tomorrow I'm going to fast until dinner.

Sound familiar? Guess what. This approach does not create any sort of path to real (or lasting) change. It may stun and shame you into submission for a while, but no one wants to live under the thumb of this angry judgmental attitude forever.

The first step in the rescue plan is to start sharpening your curiosity.

To be curious is to be interested. It's about wondering and seeking to understand. The nature of curiosity is openness—to learning something new, to seeing something differently, to exploring the unknown. If you look at the above example again, you won't find any of that.

Criticism and judgment are, by nature, closed, tight and narrow. When we're in a judgmental mindset, we've already drawn the conclusion about what happened and what we think about it. We're not open to understanding the situation differently; we've already summed it up. When we are the object of our own critical judgment, there is little or no self-nurturing or self-respect, and usually no effort to understand the "why" of why we chose the course of action that we did. This kind of judgment is like getting hit over the head with a blunt object.

Here's a possible conversation from the perspective of curiosity:

Wow. You ate all that cheesecake. You started out just to have a bite and now it's almost gone. Okay, deep breath. How do you feel? Gross and too full. Wow—you are really mad at yourself. Hold on. What if I take a step back? What if I try to understand this instead of beating myself up? What happened? I feel like I totally lost control. Was I hungry? You know, I don't even know if I was hungry. Well that's interesting... how come I didn't pay attention to that? I've been working so hard at the way that I eat and I've been really feeling successful all week. Hmm... what was different about tonight? Well, I was busy all day and skipped lunch, so I guess I probably was pretty hungry when I got home. What else? I was having that argument with Mike on the phone when I walked in the door—and I just opened the fridge while I was talking and saw the cheesecake. Okay... so what can I do differently tomorrow? I can definitely pack a lunch and I'll check my schedule in the morning and decide ahead of time when to eat it. Also, I'm realizing that the last two times I binged like this, I was doing more than one thing at a time; I wasn't focused on thinking about whether I wanted to eat. Plus, this time I was angry. I wonder if it would help if I didn't talk on my cell in the kitchen?...

Quite a difference, right? You might even feel it physically. When I was writing the judgmental example, I realized that my shoulders were creeping up around my ears. I was clenching my jaw and holding my breath—much in the way I react when my own judgmental voice lets loose on me. I didn't realize any of this until I wrote the other example. The curious example relaxed me. I found myself taking a deep breath as I wrote it. Think about your own judgmental and curious voices. Do you use the curious voice much? Do you shine it on yourself and allow yourself to wonder about why you do what you do in a nonjudgmental way? The lack of judgment is an essential skill for gaining control over emotional eating. Judgment backs us into a corner and limits our options. Curiosity creates expansiveness of thinking and opens the doors for new possibility. That is the place where change happens.

First Eskimos, Now SCUBA Training...

What does rescue training have to do with weight loss, emotional eating and hunger? I didn't know until one of my clients pointed it out to me. She was having a hard time figuring out exactly what she hungered for and what was driving her overeating. She *had* figured out that she was getting too physically hungry before she ate and then was reacting on auto-pilot, compulsively eating sweets that she didn't particularly want until she was physically uncomfortable. We were trying to devise a strategy to slow her down so that she could tune in to herself and start to make deliberate decisions about when and how to respond to her hunger when she had an "aha" moment. "It's like underwater rescue training!"

An experienced diver, she explained to me that SCUBA divers are taught a simple formula: Stop, Breathe, Think and Act. The process is drilled into divers' heads as a way of combating the instinctive fight or flight response that can be triggered in underwater emergency situations. Divers know that instinctive responses are not the way to react in crisis because these responses are usually wrong and can be deadly. When facing a crisis situation, divers are drilled to learn to *Stop* instead of reacting instinctively. This requires no thought and starts to slow them down. The next step is to *take a slow deep Breath*. Again, this is calming. These two steps provide some time and space for the brain to engage in order to formulate a rational course of action (*Think*). Only then, with your brain on board, should you *Act*.

As you move through the book, it will be useful to keep this formula in mind. Creating a new relationship with food means taking control of old patterns and behaviors that may have become automatic and feel instinctive. This formula accurately describes the process that will allow you to make changes in your responses to hunger, in the way you eat, and ultimately in your weight.

*The Emotional Eating Rescue Plan
for Smart, Busy Women:*

Your New Tools

Curiosity

"Do not wait; the time will never be "just right." Start where you stand, and work with whatever tools you may have at your command, and better tools will be found as you go along."

—GEORGE HERBERT

"The thing that is really hard, and really amazing, is giving up on being perfect and beginning the work of becoming yourself."

—ANNA QUINDLEN

"There is a reason we overeat. Always."

—MELISSA MCCREERY

Getting Started

The first step in your rescue plan will be starting to create familiarity and a foundation with your new tools. Becoming comfortable with these tools and working through the steps this week will help you start discovering what you need to know about yourself, your appetites, your physical hunger and your relationship with food and eating so that you can put food back in its appropriate place and get on with your life.

The Rules

These are the underpinnings of the rescue plan. When all else fails, when you feel like you are lost or stuck, come back to these four principles. If you take nothing else from this program, take these. Write them down in a place where you will see them often. They are what you need to get back on track and keep moving forward.

1. Knowledge is power—never forget that *you* have a lot of knowledge. Above all, and when all else "fails," be curious. Ask yourself *what can I learn from this?*
2. Follow the SCUBA training guidelines: Stop, Breathe, Think and Act.
3. You overeat for a reason. Always. Never ignore your hunger. Identify it, respect it, and make every effort to feed yourself in the highest quality, most appropriate way.

4. Remember that change is not a one shot deal and that the process of change is seldom a straight, smooth line. It is normal to have a bumpy path with plateaus and stuck spots along the way. Usually we need to learn a lesson more (perhaps a *lot* more) than once.

The Rescue Plan

The Emotional Eating Rescue Plan for Smart, Busy Women contains a great deal of information about the tools that will allow you to stop obsessing about food, put it in its appropriate place, and get on with your life.

Learning *about* the tools and learning *how to incorporate* the tools is a process, one that you will continue to craft as you work through this plan as well as afterwards. It's a process of trial and error and of adjustments. Tell your inner-perfectionist to listen up—getting it *imperfect* (and making adjustments) is actually part of the process. *And it takes time.*

In order to get the most from the rescue plan, you will need to take a committed approach. You'll be incorporating three consistent activities into your life. These activities are fundamental to the program and will really provide you the material—the food for thought, pun intended—that you will be working on as you move through the book. Start these activities THIS WEEK. Starting new habits is challenging, and I know that adding three new habits is a lot. *The expectation is not that you'll get it perfect.* These are habits to experiment with. Be playful and be curious. Believe me, these are powerful tools. People who've completed this program find that all three activities eventually work together rather beautifully. They attribute their success with the rescue plan to learning to use all three of these tools.

To make things easier, I've created a special resource page where you can download and print worksheets, templates, and some of the tools you'll be using. If you'd like to get ahead of the game and just print these out now, go here: http://toomuchonherplate.com/eerp-resource-page/.

You'll need about 30 minutes a day to devote to the new tools that are a part of your rescue plan. Throughout the book, I will ask you to give deliberate thought to scheduling. Busy women are often tempted to skip this step or to rationalize that they will figure the schedule out later. Please don't do this!

The questions about *when* you are going to do something are important; pay attention to them. Read through all the materials for this week and spend some time with your calendar or schedule, determining how *you* can best work this program.

Scheduling the activities into your week in advance will not only increase your ability to use the tools successfully. Creating a place in your schedule for the program will also decrease your stress and make incorporating new changes easier. There's actually a third reason that scheduling yourself is important. Prioritizing your own needs and carving out time for yourself is a critical strategy that many smart, busy women neglect or believe they can't make time for. It's a huge mistake, and it's the first piece of the puzzle I'm asking you to address. Change is difficult and it's smart to use every advantage you can. So here we go—it's time to dive in.

Busy Women's Tip:

When you are busy, it can be especially challenging to fit things in—particularly new habits that aren't a part of your current routine. I recommend a few tools and tricks to make this easier on you while you work to create automatic habits.

1. Never assume your rescue plan will "just happen." I'm going to keep harping on this one because smart women like us are famous for ignoring this advice. Decide when you are going to claim the time for the rescue plan and claim it. Don't try to tack this on at the end of the day when you are exhausted. Claim a time when you are fresh and have energy.

2. Use reminders. Schedule yourself on your calendar, and set an alarm on your phone or computer to remind you of it. Create mental cues or motivators: a quotation on a sticky note that reminds you why the rescue plan is a priority or a song on your playlist that motivates you to take time for you.

3. Reward yourself. Starting something new can be difficult and awkward. It really does take 21 days to create a habit, so give yourself lots of credit and compassion while you work up to this goal. Rewarding ourselves is another area where busy women often short-change themselves, but prizes and celebrations can be great motivators. Decide how you will honor completing each week of the program. What lovely thing can you promise yourself?

Sunday: Day 1

For purposes of consistency, each week of this program will begin on a Sunday. For many people, the weekend is a good time to get organized and scheduled for the week ahead. When you are busy all week, the weekend can be a great place to catch your breath, define your priorities, and get purposeful about the coming week. Of course, if another format works better for you, adjust the days of the week in the rescue plan accordingly.

Week one is about creating a solid foundation. If you haven't already done so, read the first chapter: *Creating Real Change*. Then read through this chapter. When you are finished reading, you are going to develop your personal rescue plan schedule for the rest of the week.

After you have read the materials, go to the chart at the end of the chapter and record your Master Schedule for the week ahead. Remember—scheduling yourself is a way of setting priorities. It's a critical step in the rescue plan. The activities that you schedule will be your assignments for the next seven days.

Step One: Slowing Down and Paying Attention

Living busy, over-scheduled lives, it is far too easy to get stuck in a pattern of being reactive—doing the next thing that needs to be done, following our schedule, one frenzied step at a time, instead of looking ahead and charting our course.

If we are not paying good attention, we are more likely to put a bandage on current problems instead of taking the time to create a real, lasting fix. When we are not paying attention and choosing a deliberate course of action, we tend to react instinctively. Sometimes this can even feel like acting on autopilot. If we're accustomed to using food as one of those automatic responses, not paying attention is going to set us up to use food as that bandage.

When we live in a state of non-attention for long periods of time, we become disconnected from our priorities, our values, our hearts, our spirits and our bodies.

Mindfulness is the state of being present, of *being* fully in the moment. It is the method of purposefully paying attention in the present without judgment and with curiosity.

It is the practice of fully being in your life and in your body, and this mindfulness is a fundamental goal of your rescue plan. Learning how to be more connected (and get reconnected when you fall off track) is a major strategy you'll be using to end your struggles with emotional eating and with food.

When we are able to connect with ourselves in a mindful way, we know, in that moment, who we are. We know what is important, what we are worried about, what hurts, what needs stretching. We know whether we are hungry or tense or happy or overwhelmed.

When we know these things, we can figure out how to take care of ourselves much more effectively.

The consequences of NOT being mindful

When we're not fully mindful (as can easily happen when we're overbooked or overwhelmed), it means our lives don't have our full attention. We're not operating consciously. When we're busy, multi-tasking, or distracted, it's easy to sense a need, a problem or a feeling and respond to it inappropriately—just to do SOMETHING. Not being mindful is likely to lead to an instinctive reaction.

We're worried so we snap at our spouse. We're tired, but we mislabel it as hunger and eat half a roll of cookie dough without really noticing. Work is unrewarding, so we come home and zone out while we watch mindless TV (or eat the other half of the cookie dough). We're stressed so we go shopping. We get reactive, defensive. We tend to do more things to "escape," "get numb," or distract ourselves. We become preoccupied with something, anything, which really has nothing to do with what's going on with us. Often, that something is food.

To make matters worse, there is a vicious cycle at work here. Not being mindful or aware, begets *more* of that same distracted and disconnected mental state.

Cultivating your piece of quiet

Creating more mindfulness has two parts.

1. We need to know how to create a state of mindfulness in the midst of stress and chaos.
2. We need some kind of regular practice so we can get better at staying connected and being mindful in our day-to-day lives.

My five minute tip for mindfulness

One thing at a time. That's it. It's quick and simple. Mindfulness is about *being present*. It doesn't matter what you are doing, but the rule is you can do and think about only one thing at a time and you keep your mind on that thing. You put the load of laundry in and keep your mind focused on exactly what you are doing. No judgment, no critiquing, no getting three steps ahead of yourself. You do what you are doing. You focus on experiencing it with all your senses. You breathe deeply.

Try washing the dishes this way. It will slow down your heart rate if you do it mindfully. Try eating a mindful meal. Sitting down. Food on a plate. Notice how it looks and smells. Chew it carefully. Notice how your body feels as you feed it. Can you tell when you are full?

This five-minute tip is great to use when you are in the middle of being really busy and you suddenly realize how agitated and out of control it feels. It's effective because it slows you down and helps you focus on what is happening and what you are experiencing. It's do-able because it doesn't require you to stop or be completely still. Sometimes when you are stressed, busy or agitated, the idea of completely stopping or quieting your mind can seem like trying to put toothpaste back in the tube—impossible and extremely messy. This five-minute mindfulness tip works and will help you be present in your life.

Mindfulness is *not* solely about meditation

Mindfulness meditations are a great way to focus inward and be present with your mind and body. To practice mindfulness meditation, sit quietly, focus your awareness on your breath, and watch your thoughts without attachment or judgment. You do "nothing" and you stay present. As thoughts float through your mind or your focus drifts, you "notice" the phenomenon and then you gently bring your attention back to your breathing. No judgment. If you think you'd like to try meditation, please do. Find a quiet place where you can relax undisturbed and start with 10 minutes a day. This kind of practice will help you become more centered and can be a wonderful way to begin your morning.

For many, meditation feels too foreign, too overwhelming, or just awkward. That's fine. Respect what you know about yourself. Don't set yourself up to do something you know you won't do. The real key is finding a way of connecting to yourself that works for you and that honors who you are. Do you need to get quiet? Connect with your body? Be in nature? Move or be still?

You are seeking something that *puts you in the moment*, something that *connects you with yourself*, that calms you and focuses and sharpens your senses. Here are some ideas for activities that, when done with intention, can deepen mindfulness:

Journaling

Drawing (or coloring)

Practicing yoga

Running or walking

Meditation

Deep breathing

Gardening

Sitting

Holding a sleeping child or a purring cat

Playing an instrument

Drinking tea

Taking a bath

Dancing

Washing windows

I'm sure you'll have more ideas as you ponder the idea of mindfulness. Take an inventory of how much "mindful time" you have in your life. Are there activities you could add that sound appealing? Are there times of day when you regularly have to pry yourself off the ceiling—where a mindfulness ritual might help you take better care of yourself?

This week, try an experiment. Try doing something mindfully for at least 10 minutes three or four times a week. Notice how it feels. Notice what you struggle with, what you enjoy. Try to stay curious and nonjudgmental about it.

Make some notes here:

Mindful activities that are already a part of my life on a regular basis:

_____

_____

_____

_____

This week, I will try the following mindful activity (choose a new activity or commit to a regular schedule of a mindful activity that you already do):

_____

_____

_____

_____

SMART TOOLS: The Success Soundtrack™

Busy women who have a lot on their plates often have a difficult time slowing down or taking time for themselves. You may find that this is a challenge for you and that you could benefit from some extra help.

When you've been functioning in overdrive for a while, slowing down, doing one thing at a time, or really focusing on being present with yourself might not feel natural or comfortable. It might even feel selfish or like it's a waste of time. Sometimes, busy people find that they just don't know *what to do* if they actually stop and try to take the time.

If you are a successful person who is used to having all the answers, this may feel kind of silly. Never fear— you aren't alone!

Taking the time and allowing yourself a few minutes of mindfulness can be so challenging, that I developed a tool specifically for high-achieving women who struggle in this area. The Success Soundtrack™ is a fully downloadable program that gives you a series of 10 minute audios, each with a different focus, but all of which focus you on YOU. All you need to do is download these to your mp3 player or computer, put on your headphones, choose a 10 minute soundtrack for the day, and listen. It's an easy "autopilot" way to develop a mindfulness habit. This handy tool also includes a complete hour-long session on many of the mindset traps that can sabotage smart, busy high-achievers and lead to problems with emotional eating.

You can find out more about the program at http://toomuchonherplate.com/successsoundtrack/

Commit to days and times. Write them on your calendar and your Master Schedule for the week (at the end of the chapter) as well.

_____

_____

_____

_____

Step Two: Your Journal

Your journal is an important tool in the rescue plan. To get started, you'll need something you can write in, and you'll need to feel 100 percent secure about the confidentiality of what you write. This is extremely important. You won't be able to unload your brain if you are worried about whether it's safe to do it. I tell my coaching clients to do whatever it takes to feel sure that their writing is private. If it requires locking your journal in the trunk of your car every night— go for it.

You can choose to write either the old fashioned way, on paper, or on your computer. I recommend journaling by hand because it seems to have a different kind of impact than typing on a keyboard. That said, go with the approach that works for you and with which you will follow through.

As part of the rescue plan, you'll be spending 15 minutes every day writing in your journal. Don't let this intimidate you. You don't have to re-read what you write, it doesn't have to be grammatically correct, and this is not a log of everything you ate in the last 24 hours. The guidelines are simple. Sit down in a comfortable place and write. Write about whatever is on your mind, even if it is "I don't have anything to write about."

Write with curiosity. If you are beating yourself up in your writing, stop for a moment, take notice, then write with curiosity about THAT (*"why am I being so hard on myself?"*). Write without an agenda of what you are "supposed" to be accomplishing. You are writing to write. You are writing to see what comes out on the paper when you give yourself space. You are writing to get into the habit (or strengthen the habit) of slowing down and communicating with yourself. You are writing to get stuff out of your head and down on paper.

If you haven't been in the habit of doing this kind of writing, you may find it's similar to biking with rusty gears. At first it feels clunky and awkward as the gears get unstuck and begin slowly to move again. Over time, as the gears begin to mesh, as the rust "un-sticks" and the movement begins to disperse the necessary lubrication, the gears will begin moving with much less effort—as they were meant to do. The habit of daily writing can be one of the most powerful tools for making sure that you are not going hungry in any area of your life. It's not unusual for it to become something you will eagerly anticipate.

Your rescue plan journaling checklist:

- Buy or find a notebook to use. (Writing by hand works better for most people than using a computer. If you choose to use technology instead, designate a specific folder or place to store your writing.)

- Designate a time of day to write. Morning works best for many people. I suggest that you don't write at bedtime: sometimes writing stirs up thoughts and feelings and this can interfere with sleep.
- If you have avoided writing in the past because you find that emotions come to the surface and leave you feeling uncomfortable, start with writing 5-10 minutes a day, three times a week. Schedule some kind of activity directly after your writing session so that you are immediately distracted by that activity. It could be going for a walk or running errands, but make sure it is something that moves you to another location for at least a brief period of time.

Your rescue plan:

I will write in my journal _____ days a week for _____ minutes. I will do it at the following time of day _____.

Make sure that you also schedule this on your Master Schedule for the week at the end of this chapter.

Step Three: The ME Log™ (Mindful Eating Log)

The ME Log™ is a powerful component of this program.

Before you stop reading and run away, read the next sentence. **I am not asking you to keep a food diary.** I'm not asking you to measure your starches, count your carbs or calories or potato chips. What I AM asking you to do is track *the process* of your hunger and how you respond to it. Many food plans, dieticians and diet "experts" ask you to track your food intake in excruciating detail. While I understand *why* they do it, I can count on fewer than two hands the number of individuals I've worked with in 20 years of practice who enjoyed doing this.

The exercise that I'm asking you to do is quite different. I am asking you to slow down (*Stop. Breathe*,) and *Think* (remember the SCUBA divers' mantra?) about the when, why and how of your eating. Using the ME Log™ will help you do all of these things. It will also give you a useful record to examine if you get curious about patterns or timing or anything else related to your eating.

Make a commitment to complete the ME Log™ for at least three days in the next week. If you can do it more frequently, all the better. This is a method of gathering data about yourself and your relationship with food. The more data you have, the more you can learn. Please remember—*this is not a Judgment Log*. There are no right or wrong answers, and you can't pass or fail. This is a curiosity exercise. We're collecting data that will be helpful to you in both the short and long term.

The ME Log™ has eight rows (plus an extra row for your comments and thoughts). Each row has a specific purpose which I'll describe below.

Time

This row is pretty straightforward. It's where you note what time it was when you ate something. Don't get too hung up on it—it's not important whether it was noon or 12:07. What you want is something that will help you pinpoint the approximate time of day. Again, this can help you recall the event and identify patterns later on.

What I ate

Again, this is not a calorie log. You don't need to measure or be overly precise unless tracking your portion size is important to you. Recording "Steak and Green Beans" would be fine. What you are taking note of here is how you chose to feed yourself.

What I was doing

What were you doing when you realized you were hungry? Were you cleaning the bathroom, talking on the phone, fighting with your boyfriend? If you ate without thinking about hunger, what were you doing immediately prior to making the decision to eat? If you were multi-tasking while eating, make a note about what you were doing then as well (i.e. "sitting at my desk answering emails").

How I was feeling (an emotion)

This is a tough one for some people. So be patient with yourself as your brain gets used to being asked about your emotions before getting hungry or before eating. When people eat to cope with emotions, their goal is somehow to change or cope with a feeling that was occurring *before* they started to think about food or began to eat. It's helpful, therefore, to think about the minutes before you ate or before it occurred to you to do so.

Try to be as precise as you can about the emotion. The size of your vocabulary of feeling words is dependent on how often you think and talk about your feelings. Some people tend not to be emotionally introspective but rather think of how they are feeling as "good" or "bad." I'm going to ask you to be more precise—a LOT more precise. I've included a "cheat sheet" of feeling words, not complete by any means, that you can use to trigger your own thinking about your feelings (it's at the end of this chapter). If "good" or "bad" or "nothing" is all that you can identify at first, write this down and keep working on it. As you spend time being curious about how and what you are feeling, you will get better at identifying the feelings you are experiencing. You may even develop a whole new vocabulary!

By the way, it's not unusual to notice a certain numbness *while* you are eating. This happens to many women who zone out or go on autopilot when they eat. As you practice the SCUBA technique, this will shift, but at first you many need to focus on being patient with yourself and simply noting what you *do* know about what you were feeling just before the eating episode or the hunger occurred.

Hunger level before and after eating

This is the place where you get to be curious about your physical hunger. In these columns, you will rate your feelings of hunger on a scale of 0-10 based on the scale below. This will probably take some practice. Over time, you will get better at knowing what a 2 or a 4 or a 9 rating feels like in your body. As you start to collect this data, you can fill in your own descriptions on the scale.

Again, remember that there are no right or wrong answers when it comes to hunger. You are collecting data and exercising your curiosity muscles.

Hunger Scale

0 Famished, starving, empty
1
2
3
4
5 Neutral, not full and not hungry
6
7
8
9
10 Stuffed to the point of discomfort, painfully overfull

What I was *really* hungry for

Again, there is no "correct" answer. Take some time, take a few deep breaths, and write down what you know in this column, whatever it is. It might be that you ate salad and carrot sticks and what you were really hungry for was a baked potato. Maybe you ate half a bag of cookies and what you really wanted was your date from last Friday to call you back. Or maybe you ate grilled cheese with your three year old and what you were really hungry for was shrimp scampi. This is not a "should" column as in "what my diet mentality says I should have eaten." This is an "identifying what you really hungered for" column.

A note here: if you are accustomed to dieting, your brain may have a hard time wrapping itself around the idea of thinking about what it really wants. If you are dealing with a long history of deprivation, it will be normal to find a brain really hungry for indulgence or decadence. Don't let this scare you and take special care here with how much latitude you let your judgmental mind have. If you find yourself lapsing into critical negative judgment, keep gently nudging yourself back into a mindset of curiosity. You're collecting data so that you can learn more about you and how to take care of yourself in good ways. Nothing more.

How I felt after eating (an emotion)

This may be a new one for you to think about. Your job is to identify an emotion, not a physical state like "full." If you find yourself writing *guilty* or *ashamed* or an emotion related to feeling badly about how you have eaten, spend some time investigating whether there are any other emotions there. Write down everything you discover. Again, don't worry if you find yourself drawing a blank at first. Open your mind to the question, and allow yourself to keep playing with it.

It's time for some action. Let's create your Accountability Plan.

Your plan:

I will keep my ME Log™ on the following days next week (make sure you also enter this in your Master Schedule for the week):

_____

_____

Master Schedule for Week One

Days 1–7	Date	Mindfulness (list the mindful activity and the time you have scheduled it)	Journaling (record the time of day you will do this)	ME Log™ (check the days that you will complete)
Sunday				
Monday				
Tuesday				
Wednesday				
Thursday				
Friday				
Saturday				

_____

_____

_____

It's a good time to review the rules of the program:

1. Knowledge is power—remember that you have a great deal of knowledge. Above all, and when all else "fails," be curious. Ask yourself _what can I learn from this?_
2. Follow the SCUBA training guidelines: Stop, Breathe, Think and Act.
3. You overeat for a reason. Always. Never ignore your hunger. Identify it, respect it, and make every effort to feed yourself in the highest quality, most appropriate way.
4. Remember that change is not a one shot deal and that the process of change is seldom a straight, smooth line. It is normal to have a bumpy path with plateaus and stuck spots along the way. We usually need to learn a lesson more (a lot more) than once.

Week One Review:

There's no way around it. This week there is a fair amount of information to digest and new tools to discover. Try not to get overwhelmed. Remember that you can revisit this chapter any time you need. This is the information you need to get started and to begin to build a solid foundation for knowing what you really hunger for. You'll be using this information to learn how to feed yourself in the highest quality ways (not just your stomach, but your soul and your spirit too), and take charge of emotional eating and overeating.

The theme for the week is *curiosity vs. judgment*. If the going gets challenging, it might be a good time to step back and see if you need to be less judgmental and more curious with whatever you are doing.

Your Action Plan:

1. Copy the rules of the rescue plan and put them somewhere where you will see them often.
2. Commit to a mindfulness activity on specific days and times this week (at least three times for at least 10 minutes each time). Schedule those and record them on your Master Schedule and on your calendar or in your schedule.
3. Find a journal. Commit to writing in it three to seven times a week for 5-15 minutes (aim for 15 minutes). Commit to a time of day to do this and schedule it.
4. Commit to keeping the ME Log™ at least three days over the next week. Check your schedule and pick days that will work for you and your lifestyle.
5. When in doubt, be curious!

Put It in Writing:

I will commit to make every effort to be curious and not judgmental about myself and my eating during the following week. I know that I am much more likely to learn the things I need to learn about my real hungers and my needs if I am open and curious than if I am judgmental and frustrated.

I give myself permission to feel confused or unclear about things—my job over the next week is to collect data about my hunger and my eating—not to draw conclusions or know what to do with the data.

I will also write in my journal in the way I have committed and will follow the mindfulness practices I have designed for myself.

Signed: _____

*Date:*_____

The ME Log™

Time:								
What I ate:								
What I was doing:								
What I was feeling (an emotion):								
Hunger level before eating:								
Hunger level after eating:								
What I was really hungry for (a specific food or something else):								
How I felt after eating:								
Comments or observations:								

** *You'll want to make copies of this form*
You can download a copy of this form for your personal use here: http://toomuchonherplate.com/melog.pdf

Feelings "Cheat Sheet"

Absorbed	Discouraged	Humorous	Resentful
Agitated	Disgusted	Hurt	Restful
Alarmed	Distrustful	Impatient	Restless
Alert	Down	Infuriated	Sad
Alienated	Dramatic	Interested	Safe
Aloof	Eager	Irritated	Secure
Amazed	Ecstatic	Jealous	Self-conscious
Amused	Edgy	Kind	Shocked
Angry	Empowered	Lethargic	Startled
Animated	Engaged	Lighthearted	Stressed
Antsy	Engrossed	Lively	Strong
Anxious	Enraged	Loving	Supported
Appreciated	Enthusiastic	Mellow	Surprised
Aroused	Excited	Motivated	Suspicious
Ashamed	Expectant	Ornery	Sympathetic
Awe-struck	Fascinated	Outraged	Tearful
Baffled	Fatigued	Overjoyed	Tender
Blue	Flustered	Overwhelmed	Tense
Bored	Frazzled	Panicked	Tentative
Calm	Furious	Passionate	Thankful
Centered	Gay	Passive	Tired
Cold	Giddy	Playful	Touched
Compassionate	Glib	Peaceful	Troubled
Confident	Gloomy	Peeved	Uneasy
Confused	Grateful	Perplexed	Unsure
Content	Grounded	Perturbed	Vexed
Cranky	Guarded	Powerful	Warm
Curious	Guilty	Proud	Wary
Dark	Happy	Puzzled	Weary
Dazed	Heavy-hearted	Quiet	Willful
Dejected	Hopeful	Rattled	Wistful
Depraved	Hopeless	Relaxed	Worried
Depressed	Horrified	Relieved	Zany

Meeting Your Needs
without Turning to Food

"We keep moving forward, opening new doors, and doing new things, because we're curious and curiosity keeps leading us down new paths."

—WALT DISNEY

Whether you've arrived at the second week of your rescue plan feeling like you have a gold star on your forehead, or feeling a little behind or confused after last week, it's still all good. You made it. Last week was a challenge—I know that. Starting new habits doesn't usually come easily or automatically—or perfectly. And sometimes trying to do things differently just leaves us confused and irritable. It happens. But trying out the new habits, in whatever form you were able to make a start last week, was big. This week, we'll start where you are, and build on it.

The Rescue Plan

Read through the material for the week before you dive in. Again, there is a lot to digest here. It's all designed to give you information about yourself from which you can learn.

The material you'll be working on this week is *more* than a week's worth of material, so go at your own pace. You'll be chewing on the questions in this section for at least the next two weeks. I hope that you'll also come back to this material a month or six months from now and discover even more information about yourself. Also, keep an eye on your inner perfectionist. He or she will only get in your way, because, in answering these questions, there is no "perfect" or "right" answer. When you look at the material, focus on identifying what you know and work at being curious about what you don't.

Sunday: Day 8

This week, you are going to maintain the same three habits—**mindfulness time** for 10 minutes a day, **journaling** for 15 minutes a day, and the **ME Log™** for 3-7 days a week. In addition, you'll have daily rescue plan assignments to work on as you move through the chapter.

Change is not a one-shot-deal and neither is developing a new habit. You'll continue to get more comfortable with these activities as your rescue plan progresses. As you work to make them a part of your schedule and daily routine, you will learn some things about what works—and what doesn't. The goal is to be *curious* about the process and allow yourself to use what you learn to make adjustments, so that the things you are doing work for you and fit your needs.

Take the time to schedule your journaling, your mindful activities and your ME Log™ now. Review the week ahead and plan when these activities will fit on your calendar. Take some time to review any hurdles you came up against with scheduling or with accomplishing these activities (remember to be curious, not judgmental). What would make it easier to be successful over the next week? Are there things you learned from your experience last week that would be helpful to take into consideration over the week ahead?

Write any thoughts or notes about that here:

_____

_____

_____

_____

_____

_____

_____

_____

_____

_____

_____

_____

Master Schedule for Week Two

Days 8–14	Date	Mindfulness (list the mindful activity and the time you have scheduled it)	Journaling (record the time of day you will do this)	ME Log™ (check the days that you will complete)
Sunday				
Monday				
Tuesday				
Wednesday				
Thursday				
Friday				
Saturday				

Analyzing Your Data

When I am coaching a client, I'll usually have her play around with the ME Log™ for a week or so and then we'll meet or get on the phone and talk about it. In fact, we'll spend quite a bit of time talking about it. Whether you realize it or not, by keeping this log for 3-7 days, you've collected a tremendous amount of data about your relationship with food. We certainly want to respect the hard work that you are doing collecting data by spending the time it takes to understand it. This requires some effort, and it will probably demand more practice experimenting with the ME Log™ and with the other mindful activities you are doing.

We'll spend a few weeks analyzing data—and you'll be continuing to collect more. It may take a while to be able to respond to some of the questions, and that's okay. Also, you may find that you give one set of answers this week and have additional thoughts or things to add next week. That is perfectly fine as well.

Don't try to keep this section too neat and orderly. Work through the material in the style that works best for you. You may want to read it all over first and start with whatever grabs your attention. Or, answer the "easy" questions first. You might want to set aside 15 minutes a day to work through the material. If some parts completely stump you, leave them blank, put the questions in the back of your brain and let them percolate. Notice if anything comes up.

Remember, this isn't an exam. As far as the rescue plan goes, what you *don't know* is as important as what you *do* know. "Why don't I know that?" is often an enlightening question to ask.

Busy Women's Tip:

Sometimes working harder isn't really working smarter.

High-achieving, successful people tend to have a few things in common: We're hard working and we're used to doing difficult things. We tend to be good at persevering, and we tend to expect a lot from ourselves. We're tough cookies, and we can be big thinkers.

These strengths serve us well in many areas of our lives, but they can really trip us up and even become emotional eating and overeating traps if we're not careful.

With all our big expectations and our be-tough attitude, it's tempting to dive in in a BIG way. Sometimes, we expect so much of ourselves, that we get overwhelmed before we ever start. This leads to dread, procrastination, feeling frustrated with ourselves and ultimately, NOT getting where we want to go.

This week you are going to be thinking a lot about "steps you can take." I have a tip for you.

Keep your high-achiever in check.

There is no prize or glory for designing the biggest, boldest goals or action steps this week. You don't get any points for doing something "every single day" or wearing yourself out. The prize, the learning, and the real lasting change comes when you design steps you can actually take, and keep taking, in the midst of your busy life.

Do-able, reasonable changes are the ones we are all most likely to stick with and the ones that have the best odds of growing into habits. Busy, smart, successful women tend to devalue the importance of small steps and judge themselves for "not doing enough."

Don't let that be you! This week, have the courage to be honest and realistic about the changes and challenges you can accept. Small steps move mountains—as long as you can keep taking them.

Make notes in the margins, highlight things of interest, and feel free to come back and add more to your thoughts or write in your own questions. Give your brain permission to really chew on this stuff!

_____

_____

_____

_____

_____

Which was the hardest row in the log to complete?

_____

_____

_____

_____

_____

The easiest?

_____

_____

_____

What did you learn about yourself? Did anything surprise you?

_____

_____

_____

Did completing the ME Log™ affect how you ate in any way?

_____

_____

_____

Are there things you'd like to do differently or learn more about after looking at your data?

_____

_____

_____

Monday: Day 9

Let's look more closely at each row in the ME Log™ and at the data you collected. This week, you'll want to have the ME Logs™ that you've completed in front of you so that you can examine them as we work through the categories.

Time

What can you discover about yourself and your eating patterns from reviewing *when* you ate? Do you eat at the same times every day? If so, what determines the time that you eat? Are you truly hungry for lunch at 12:30 every afternoon, or is that when you're able to take a break from your work and eat? *Remember, there are no right answers here—just data.* No need to draw any conclusions yet.

Are there certain times of day when your eating is consistent and other periods in the day when what and how much you eat varies? Is your eating evenly distributed throughout the day? Are there a few periods of eating (like meals), or is the eating more frequent, even constant? What is the largest span of time that you tend to go without eating (other than for sleep)? What time span between eating seems to suit you the best—or does this vary from day to day? Are there other thoughts or patterns that come to mind as you look at this data?

_____

_____

_____

What I Ate

How was it for you answering this question about food? This question can push buttons and stir up emotions for many women. The culture of dieting and weight loss gets us so focused on making value judgments about what we put in our mouths. When those value judgments become rigid and narrow, food gets divided into "good" or "bad," and eating can become a desperate struggle to be "virtuous." This is a painful pattern in which to get caught. Because there is little to no middle ground, people become stuck in excruciating cycles of rigid, depriving eating periods (diets) alternating with periods of rebellion and reaction to the extreme and unrealistic expectations these diets place on the body and soul. When food is "good" or "bad," the non-dieting periods (eating "bad" food) may never be truly enjoyed, because eating certain foods has become connected with feeling guilt, shame or embarrassment.

If parts of this pattern ring true for you, you might find that writing down what you ate was accompanied by feelings of pride or shame or guilt. It may have been difficult to record anything in response to this prompt. Some of us become so uncomfortable or weary with our attempts to lose weight or maintain a weight loss that the whole idea of *what I ate* brings up confusion or leaves us feeling overwhelmed or like it's "never right." Others may eat with defiance—"I'll eat what I want, thank you very much." Still others may find themselves confused by this whole discussion—"what feelings? I just filled in the column."

Another interesting piece of data related to this category is how easy or difficult it was to report your food in terms of being aware or remembering what you ate. People have different styles. Did you fill in this part of the ME Log™ with the food on your plate, before a bite touched your lips? Are you now saying "what plate?" Did you complete this row after eating? If so, did you do it right away or did you put it off? Did you have a hard time recalling what you ate, or could you report it to the ounce? What level of attention do you pay to what you actually eat?

Write your thoughts and impressions about the data here or in your journal:

_____

_____

_____

_____

_____

_____

_____

_____

_____

_____

_____

_____

Tuesday: Day 10

Today we keep analyzing the data you've collected with your ME Log™ thus far.

What I Was Doing

What kind of patterns or trends do you see when you pay attention to what you were doing when the hunger struck? What were you doing before you ate and were you multi-tasking (yes, watching TV or checking your email count as multitasking) while you ate? Was what you were doing before you ate related to your decision to eat?

Here's an example from my own life that you might find helpful. I often have chocolate in my office. I can go for days at a time without even remembering it's there. Other days, I am reaching for it all day long. I am usually not more physically hungry on the days when I can't leave the chocolate alone. If I stop and pay attention to my hunger, my activities, and their relationship to the chocolate I'm eating, I usually find that I am feeling overwhelmed in some way—facing a problem I haven't yet figured out how to address, feeling time crunched or tired. At those moments, I'll often reach for the chocolate *instead* of picking up the phone and making the difficult phone call or *before* I dive in to the looming pile of paperwork or *instead of* taking a break. It's a delay and a comfort tactic. *If* I stop and notice this and also notice that I am not actually physically hungry for chocolate, and *if* I address the feeling and/or dive into the activity (telling myself that I can have the chocolate *afterward*), I usually forget about the chocolate entirely.

What do you notice about your activity patterns and how they relate to eating? By the way, you may want to revisit this section after examining your data on hunger levels.

_____

_____

_____

_____

_____

_____

_____

_____

_____

_____

_____

_____

_____

_____

_____

How I Was Feeling

What was it like to tune in to your emotions? Was it difficult or easy? Were your responses varied or did it feel monotonous—you found yourself writing the same emotion over and over? Double-check this row and make sure that what you really wrote down were *emotions*. It's not uncommon to find it difficult to come up with an actual feeling or to discover that although you think you did, when you examine your answers, a lot of them aren't really emotions. "Good" and "Bad" aren't feelings! Don't forget to use your cheat sheet if you come up blank here.

If you find that you really didn't (or couldn't) note your emotions or feelings in this row, ask *why* that happened. (Remember, curiosity not judgment!) What might be going on here? Can you get any closer to identifying a feeling by doing this detective work?

As you look at the emotions that you listed in your ME Log™, do you see any relationship between the feelings and your choice to eat at that particular time? In each instance, ask yourself whether you were feeding physical hunger or an emotional hunger or need.

It's important to note that analyzing data is a process and it goes differently each time you do it. You might be someone who fills out your log and has an "Aha!" moment of recognition even as you are completing it. You might be feeling confused as you look at your log and see scattered responses that don't form a clear pattern. You might be starting to see the glimmer of an idea of something important in your data, but it's not clear yet exactly what it is. You might be feeling judgmental about yourself and your eating and start to think "this program isn't going to work for me." All these thoughts are normal and a part of the process.

Note your thoughts and reactions, jot them down in your journal, and be *curious* about them. Work to keep the door to your curiosity open.

Write any observations about the feelings you had while eating here or in your journal. Remember, these are observations, ideas, thoughts and impressions. You don't have to defend them or draw any solid conclusions.

_____

_____

_____

_____

_____

_____

_____

_____

_____

_____

_____

_____

The Power of Curiosity

Carla (not her real name) joined one of my online emotional eating programs because she was frustrated with herself and her ongoing struggles with overeating and her weight. In fact, she was fed up. When I met her and asked her to describe what was going on, she was stuck deep in "judgmental" mode.

"I'm just lazy and I've lost my discipline. I feel like I have no control anymore. All I do is eat. I nibble at candy and stuff around the house all day long."

Carla owned her own business and worked from home. Over the previous few months, she'd found that her daytime snacking and nibbling had gotten more out of control than ever before. At the point she joined my program, the eating felt almost constant. "I am always eating. I'm never hungry. I can't remember the last time I was hungry. But that doesn't stop me. It gets worse after lunch and it just goes on and on until I go to bed at night. It's disgusting."

Carla was mad at herself and saw herself as lazy and unmotivated. She thought her struggles were "dumb" and "silly" and found the fact that she couldn't solve such a "simple problem" even more frustrating.

Here's the thing. Carla was anything *but* lazy. She had a huge amount of responsibility including her thriving business and her family and handled it all pretty masterfully, and she was busy all the time. I asked Carla to consider accepting the idea that there was a reason and a purpose behind her eating. During the week in the program in which Carla participated, I covered some ways to start using curiosity to explore what those reasons might be. When we met again a week later, Carla had a lot to share.

To start with, she wasn't feeling out of control with her eating anymore.

"Everything has changed. I started paying attention to what I was feeling before I ate. I thought I was just busy, but what I discovered using curiosity really surprised me. It turns out I'm bored. *I'm really bored.*" Carla went on to share how her small home-based business had taken off in the last few years. She'd become quite successful and was bringing in a very good income—one on which her family counted. The problem was, as financially lucrative as the work was, Carla was bored out of her mind—and there was more. When she used the curiosity tools I had given her, she realized she felt trapped.

She actually had some exciting ideas for growing her business, but she was concerned this might mean risking her secure income. Furthermore, she was worried about the stress it might add to her family if she tried to change anything, so she tried not to think about the adjustments she wanted to make. When she started to feel dissatisfied, her automatic response was to tell herself she "should" be happy. Eating was helping to distract her from her boredom and dissatisfaction and stifle the thoughts, ideas and dreams she had for her business.

As soon as Carla realized what was going on, she knew something had to change. For Carla, it was like a flipping a switch. In the week since I'd spoken to Carla, she'd not only understood what was triggering her overeating, she'd been able to put it into words and share it with others. When she talked with her husband, she'd also begun to figure out some ways for her work to evolve without putting the income at risk. The woman who had sounded depressed and frustrated the week before was excited and energetic. And no longer snacking all day.

"I joined this program because I wanted to lose weight," she said. "I had no idea that I would end up changing my life."

Wednesday: Day 11

Today I'd like you to take a look at the data you've collected around your hunger.

Hunger Level (before and after eating)

Noting the level of your physical hunger, both before and after eating, is a huge step to take. If you aren't accustomed to tuning in to your physical hunger, it can also be difficult to identify and to gauge. Here are some points to be curious about:

How do you identify when you are physically hungry? Where do you feel it in your body?

_____

_____

_____

_____

_____

_____

_____

_____

_____

_____

_____

_____

Here is the Hunger Scale again. It's useful to try filling in the blank, unlabeled lines with descriptions that fit your hunger (i.e. describe is a "1" or a "4"). Again, don't be surprised if it's difficult or if you don't immediately know the answers. The things you don't know might give you information about those things that need your attention.

0 Famished, starving, empty
1
2
3
4
5 Neutral, not full and not hungry
6
7
8
9
10 Stuffed to the point of discomfort, painfully overfull

Within what range do you tend to keep your physical hunger? Does it range from 0 to 10, 2 to 5 or 5 to 9?

_____

_____

_____

What hunger or fullness level feels most comfortable for you? Are there places on the hunger scale that feel uncomfortable? Are there levels of hunger or fullness that you never allow yourself to feel? Other thoughts or observations?

_____

_____

_____

_____

_____

_____

_____

_____

_____

_____

Have there been periods in your life when you kept your physical hunger/fullness in a different range than you do now? What was that range and what did it feel like?

_____

_____

_____

_____

_____

_____

Here are some things we know about feeding physical hunger. People tend to feel the most "evenly fed" if they aim to stay within a range of 3 (hungry, ready to eat) to 7 (comfortably full, satisfied) with their hunger. Staying within this range means learning to listen carefully to your body so that you can recognize when you are beginning to feel hungry and learn to stop eating when you are "just full enough."

Allowing yourself to get too hungry (and your blood sugar to get too low) will predispose you physiologically to overeat or to go for "quick fix" foods that will raise your blood glucose levels rapidly. Conversely, eating to a point of being uncomfortably full can lead to a cycle of restricting the next day.

Can you recognize a hunger level of "3" and a fullness level of "7?" Collect some data over the next few days and record your observations here. Note the physical sensations you feel (or cease to feel) with these levels of hunger and fullness:

For me, a 3 feels like:

_____

_____

_____

For me, a 7 feels like:

_____

_____

_____

If you decided to aim to keep your hunger within the range of 3-7, what changes would you need to make to the way you feed yourself or in the way you identify or listen to your hunger? List three changes here:

_____

_____

_____

_____

What would it be like to make those changes? Would you like to try any of these changes? Note your thoughts and

feelings about this and any commitments to change you
feel ready to make here:

_____

_____

_____

_____

_____

_____

_____

_____

Thursday: Day 12

Asking yourself what you are *really* hungry for can feel like a
loaded question. Let's take a look at what comes up for you
when you respond to this prompt on the ME Log™

What I Was Really Hungry For

Is it physical hunger or a psychological or emotional need
to be fulfilled? Were you hungry for food or for something
else? This is a powerful area of questioning in the ME
Log™. Be patient with yourself, and practice not judging
whatever you find yourself writing or wondering about here.

What kind of data did you collect about your real hunger or cravings? Was it difficult to stop and think about this or to answer the question? If you were physically hungry, did you feed yourself the food you were craving, or did you substitute something else? Remember, you are recording observations. Don't put pressure on yourself to draw conclusions about what it all means. What are you seeing or wondering about in the data?

Write about your observations here:

_____

_____

_____

_____

_____

_____

_____

_____

_____

_____

_____

Identifying what you are really hungry for may be quite tricky, at least at first. I promise that it will get easier. The previous rows on the ME Log™ may provide some data that helped you figure out where your hunger was coming from. Let's say you had a sudden craving for hot buttered movie popcorn. You may have written that down. Let's go a bit deeper. Were you hungry for the popcorn because your stomach didn't have any food in it—you were a "3" or even a "2" on the hunger scale and popcorn was really what you wanted to fill you up? Or—were you not really hungry at all but now that you think about it, you were kind of blue because it was a rainy day and prior to getting "hungry" you had been on a phone call where your plans got cancelled and then you couldn't reach anyone to do something with— in fact you were lonely—and the popcorn smell and taste reminds you of the fun time you had last week with your best friend...? In that case, ask yourself again what you were really hungry for. Was it something to do (an end to boredom)? Companionship? Excitement? Something else?

Recognizing emotional eating

If you aren't already familiar with the concept of emotional eating, the term refers to eating that is triggered by emotional needs: "psychological hunger" vs. physical hunger.

Here are 10 Signs that You May Be Eating Emotionally:

1. The hunger comes on suddenly and the need to eat feels urgent—physiological hunger comes on slowly and it's okay to delay eating.

2. You keep eating even if you aren't hungry any-more. The hunger doesn't go away despite the

fact that you are full. You eat to the point of physical discomfort.

3. You don't know whether you were even hungry when you ate.
4. After you eat, you realize you aren't really aware of how much you ate or how it tasted.
5. You have feelings of shame, guilt or embarrassment after eating.
6. You eat because you are bored, tired, lonely, excited—not physically hungry.
7. Hunger accompanies an unpleasant emotion— anger, hurt, fear, anxiety.
8. Emotional eating begins in your mind—thinking about food—not in your stomach.
9. You crave a specific food and won't feel content until you have that. If you are eating for physical hunger, any food will fill you up.
10. You keep eating (or grazing, or nibbling) because you just can't figure out what you are hungry *for*. *Nothing* seems to hit the spot (physical hunger goes away no matter what food you choose to fill up on).

Feeding the right appetite

Figuring out what you are *really* hungry for, especially if it isn't food, can be tricky. You may end up with some blank spots and feelings of confusion here that will take time to figure out. And, as you examine the hungers that you were able to identify, you should really work to stretch your thinking. Filling in this section may become easier with time. Or, you may find that you have a fairly easy time completing this section at first, but as you learn more about how to identify and focus on your hunger, your answers in this row grow more complex or even a bit confusing. That's normal too. Keep asking the question. The end result will be that *you* will be more powerful. As you get better at paying attention to and really *listening* to your hunger, you will get better at precisely defining what you are hungry for and feeding yourself in a way that corresponds to your craving or need.

What are you hungry for?

If you are used to defining your hunger in terms of food, this question may seem straightforward. Chocolate pudding, fried chicken, Phad Thai and Caesar salad may come to mind. Don't stop there though. Those answers may be complete, OR you may be able to go deeper. Remember that definition of hunger I gave you: hunger is a strong desire or craving. It does not have to be food-specific.

Here are some things you might be hungry for:

- Something crunchy
- Something creamy
- Something chewy
- Something to do
- Some rest
- Someone to talk to
- Food—any food—I'm starving
- Something to calm me
- Something to warm me
- Something to cool me off
- Power
- Some attention
- Touch
- Answers
- Companionship

- Something that
  pleases my senses
  (sight, smell,
  taste, texture)
- Love
- Comfort
- Calm
- A break

- Sex
- Enjoyment—easy
  pleasure
- Stress relief
- An argument
- Entertainment
- A moment of
  peace and quiet

Are you getting the idea? Spend some time making your own list of hungers. Do any of those listed above particularly resonate with you? What hungers other than a physiological hunger for fuel do you experience frequently? What are they? What triggers them? Can you recognize them immediately when they appear or only in hindsight? How do you recognize them? Can you begin to identify how they feel different from physiological hunger?

My hungers:

_____

_____

_____

_____

_____

_____

_____

_____

_____

_____

Smart Busy Woman's Bonus: Savoring

Note: you may choose to work on the following bonus sections today, or come back to them at another time.

I have a client whose favorite treat (food) is a mocha latte. When she was "dieting" she didn't have mochas and when she "fell off the wagon," she'd have one daily. I suggested to her that if mochas were really one of her favorite foods, then trying to design a lifetime plan for eating that didn't include them didn't seem very compassionate. She was more than willing to make sacrifices in other areas of her eating if it meant that she could continue to have mochas and maintain her health and weight goals, but she'd been depriving herself because she didn't believe she could lose weight *and* eat and drink what she loved. "I felt like mochas were just a bad choice."

So we talked about how much she enjoys a good mocha and about *how* she enjoys them. I asked her, "When you get your mocha, how much of the mocha would you say you taste and enjoy and experience with complete attention and focus?" In other words, I was asking her how much *of each mocha* she really savored and allowed herself to take maximum pleasure in.

My client didn't hesitate for a second before she answered. "Thirty percent. I really love the first third of the mocha. After that, it's not as warm, and it just doesn't taste as good." So I asked her what she did with the last two-thirds of her mochas.

"After I drink a little bit more than a third of it, I finish it quickly because I feel like it needs to be finished." I asked her whether, if she stopped drinking the drink at the moment she stopped savoring, she would lose any enjoyment or feel deprived. Her reaction (again it was immediate), was "probably not." So, I asked her to play around with this. I asked her to spend the next week being curious about which foods she savored and which foods she did not. I asked her to wonder about what it would be like to stop eating when she was no longer savoring food and learn to find other ways of dealing with her "inner thrifty person" who could not bear to "waste" food. You see, in reality, she was feeding an important appetite with the first 30 percent of that mocha. After that, she wasn't feeding herself at all— she was merely eating food (or, more specifically, drinking a drink) from which she wasn't taking particular enjoyment, pleasure or enrichment—and drinking extra calories that she didn't want anyway.

Rescue Plan Bonus Step

This week, pay attention to how you experience (or don't) the food that you eat. Make efforts throughout the week to be 100 percent attentive to the experience of eating. Notice the smell and the temperature of your food. Take note of whether you feel the food on your tongue. Notice whether there are particular eating-related situations in which you have difficulty staying focused and savoring. Do you need to rearrange your life in order to savor your food? Are you able to stay focused on your eating throughout the eating episode or meal? Does savoring affect the way you eat? The amount you eat?

What can you change in your life to increase the pleasure you receive from the foods that you eat?

Write your observations about your savoring experiments here:

_____

_____

_____

_____

_____

_____

_____

_____

_____

_____

_____

_____

Smart Busy Woman's Bonus: Hunger

Try this exercise. Set a timer—on your watch, your cell phone, your microwave or computer. Set the timer to go off sometime more than an hour from now. When it does, *Stop. Breathe. Think* about your hunger. What are you hungry for right now? Remember—the answer may or may not be food. How strong is that hunger? If you can identify any kind of hunger, what would be the perfect way to feed it? The sky's the limit here so think BIG.

What are you *really* craving? What would be the best possible way to satisfy the hunger or the craving that you are experiencing?

Rescue Plan Power Tool

As you keep working to get more precise about when you use food to feed your hungers, it's going to be extremely important to grow your menu of alternate ways to feed yourself. Here's one way to get started.

In the table that follows, make a list in the left-hand column of any non-food hungers you noticed during the last week—things you needed or wanted. Some possibilities might include: *rest, stress relief, down time, someone to listen to me, a chance to rant, some help.*

Now, next to each item, brainstorm ways (1 to 3 perhaps) you might try to "feed" these appetites. If you get stuck, become a bit outrageous in your brainstorming. It's fine to list some forms of nourishment that aren't really attainable right now. Let's say you were feeling like you needed relief from a stressful situation. Examples of what you might have written down include *take a break and walk around the block, put on some loud music and sing loudly, call my friend and talk for a while, take a nap or a hot shower,* or *schedule some fun play time.* There are no "correct" answers. The ultimate goal is to create a list of ways to take care of your needs and hungers that fit YOU and that don't always include food.

Your list will grow and change as you continue to make peace with food and take control of your eating. It's fine to start your list here, in this book, but be prepared for it to expand and change as you do. As you work at growing new habits, you'll probably want to put a copy of this list somewhere where you can refer to it easily in the moments when you need it.

This list is going to become one of your power tools.

Ten Strategies for Avoiding Emotional Eating

When you struggle with emotional eating, you know how powerful a bad mood or a difficult time can be. How many times have you felt completely derailed by an unexpected bad day, an awful experience or strong emotions—hurt, anger, disappointment, even boredom—that seemed to pull you magnetically to the refrigerator? It's one thing to recognize emotional eating or the fact that it's about to happen. It is another thing entirely to be able to identify some things to do *instead.*

When you get stuck, refer to this list for help.

Hungers or appetites I have noticed	Ways I could feed these hungers
Example: I was bored—hungry for something to do	Call a friend, go to the library, take a walk. Say aloud "I'm bored" instead of walking mindlessly to the kitchen.

Ten things to do with a feeling when you don't know *what* to do with it (but don't want to eat everything in sight).

1. Breathe
Sit tight. Breathe in, breathe out. Feelings come in waves. No feeling, no matter how horrible, will last forever. Breathe in. Breathe out.

2. Give yourself permission to feel it
See number one. Also, remember that no feeling is EVER bigger than you. Feel. Breathe. Remind yourself, "I am bigger than this feeling and it will pass."

3. Do something physical
Emotions impact us physically. Movement and activity can help us move the emotions through our bodies. Walking, running, dancing and punching a pillow can help us discharge built up emotion and can eventually calm us down.

4. Wallow in it
Sometimes a feeling just needs to be felt, and sometimes nothing is as therapeutic as a good cry or a time-limited "pity party." Let yourself go there. If you need to, set a time limit for when you will move on—and have another activity planned to help you refocus.

5. Call a friend
Call someone you trust who cares about you. Tell them you're overwhelmed and need a friend to lend an ear. It

helps if you can tell them whether you want advice or soothing or just someone to listen to you vent.

6. Get perspective

Whatever the situation or the emotion, ask yourself what it will look like and feel like six months from now. A year? Will it be pivotal 10 years from now? If not, it doesn't mean your feelings now aren't important. It does mean that life (and you) will go on.

7. Distract yourself

Rent a movie, play a video game, read a book, clean out a drawer, wash a window. Focus on something—anything.

8. Change your scenery

Do something—anything to shake up or change the scene. Leave the house, go for a walk or a drive, visit a museum or a book store.

9. Empower yourself

Remind yourself of your strengths. Make a list of your accomplishments. Write down all the tough situations you have survived, the exams you've taken, the children to whom you've given birth, the challenges you've conquered. Leave no stone unturned and give yourself ample credit.

10. Sleep

When you just don't feel up to anything else, give yourself a time out. Take a nap or pack it in and go to bed early.

Tomorrow is another day and often, a good night's sleep can have a huge, positive impact.

Friday: Day 13

Today will involve more work with your data from the ME Log™ and another prompt to help you get clarity on what you crave and hunger for.

How I Felt After Eating

Tuning in to your feelings before and after eating can provide important information about the emotional appetite food is feeding, in addition to your physical need for food. What kind of feeling does the eating lead to—satisfied, tired, guilty, pleased, numb?

There are three patterns that are useful in these scenarios. The "feelings" I am referring to here might be emotions such as sadness or anxiety; they also might be physical sensations such as exhaustion or physical pain.

1. **Food to enhance feelings**: One example of this is social eating. If you are out with friends or family at your favorite restaurant having a great time, and you associate the experience and the good feelings with ordering baskets of chips and margaritas, you might find yourself ordering, eating and drinking without ever even checking in with yourself about your physical hunger. In these situations, you may associate feeding

yourself food with increasing the happy emotions you're already feeling. **Notice, however, that *the eating is not connected to physical hunger.***

2. **Food to distract from feelings:** This is eating when you are trying "not to think about things" or eating to "zone out" after a stressful or difficult day. In these situations, eating is something mindless that you do to be less present in your current situation, whether it's a deadline you're facing while you munch on chocolate, a chaotic afternoon at home with the kids when you find yourself mindlessly "tasting" as you cook, or the bowl of popcorn you polish off while surfing the internet trying to forget your awful day at work. *The key word here is "mindless."*

   Eating in these situations is a way to disconnect. In the process, we usually disconnect from the eating itself. You might not even realize that you ate the whole bag of whatever-it-was. You certainly didn't savor each bite. Afterward you might feel pleasantly numb, embarrassed or ashamed as you come back to awareness and judge your eating harshly.

3. **Food to transform feelings:** This kind of eating commonly happens when you are mistaking the feeling you are having for hunger *or* if you know it isn't physical hunger but you don't know what to do about the feeling that it is. Eating because you are tired (instead of resting) is a perfect example of behavior that falls into this

category. So is "I was so mad at him that I came home and ate a pint of ice cream." Logically, we know that eating ice cream doesn't do a thing about feeling angry—but many of us have done that or something similar more times than we care to remember.

Often when we use food to transform feelings, it is because *we don't know what to do with the actual feeling we are having*. We may know we are tired, but we don't feel entitled or able to take a break and rest. We might know we're angry, but we don't know what to do with that emotion, so we also feel *powerless* and *trapped* with our anger. Consequently, we eat ice cream. **The key concept to watch for here is using food for comfort.**

As you look at the ME Logs™ you have completed, what patterns do you see with your feelings and food?

_____

_____

_____

_____

_____

_____

Are there times when you eat that are not connected to physical hunger? What do you notice about those times?

_____

_____

_____

_____

_____

_____

Are there times when you tend to eat mindlessly? Do you notice any pattern or any particular situations or feelings that tend to trigger mindless eating?

_____

_____

_____

_____

_____

_____

_____

If you have periods when you tend to eat mindlessly:

What three small changes could you make to help you be more aware of your eating? Examples here include focusing on one task at a time (no multitasking such as watching TV or browsing the Internet while eating), or remembering to put the food on a plate before eating it. Keep in mind the SCUBA maxim: Stop. Breathe. Think. And Act.

1. _____

_____

_____

2. _____

_____

_____

3. _____

_____

Now, JUST as importantly, what do you know about that feeling that you were trying to disconnect from (by eating mindlessly)? What three things could you do to start taking better care of how you were feeling?

1. _____

_____

_____

2. _____

_____

_____

3. _____

_____

_____

Are there places or times when you eat to try to transform feelings? If so, when do you notice this happening (under what circumstances)? Are there ways in which you might be more aware, or "tuned in" to the reality that this is happening?

_____

_____

_____

_____

_____

_____

_____

_____

_____

Are there particular feelings or situations to which you aren't sure how to respond and that trigger emotional eating? What are they?

_____

_____

_____

_____

_____

_____

What do you think would happen if, next time you found yourself in that situation, you were able to name it ("*I feel anxious*") and be honest about how stuck you feel? ("*I feel anxious and I don't really know what to do about it.*")?

_____

_____

_____

_____

_____

_____

Remember—it's not shameful to feel stuck. *Naming* a problem is the first step to allowing curiosity in. Curiosity is what allows us to tackle tough situations.

Saturday: Day 14

Self-care and Non-negotiables

Emotional eating is an easy trap to fall into when you aren't getting the quality care and attention that you need in other areas of your life. It's all too easy for this to happen when you are a busy woman with a lot on your plate.

At this point in the journey, it's critical to get crystal clear on what you need to function as your best version of yourself. We'll start by focusing on the bare essentials and call these your "non-negotiables"—those things that you absolutely *must* have on a regular basis in order for you to be well-nourished in the important areas of your life.

Non-negotiables are something only *you* can define. There are some things that are non-negotiable for all of us; we also each have our own unique cravings and needs. Non-negotiables go beyond the basics such as sleep and oxygen. Your non-negotiables are the things, the people, and the experiences that feed your spirit and your soul and allow you to show up with the proverbial twinkle in your eye.

It is vitally important to know what your needs for real, deep nourishment are so that you can make sure that you are getting your appetites addressed, and can develop plans for addressing any roadblocks or hurdles you might find yourself facing along the way.

Today's focus is on articulating your list of non-negotiable hungers and needs.

In order to be well fed, I need: (fill in what you know about your specific needs in each area).

Sleep:

_____

_____

Water:

_____

_____

Nutritional Needs:

_____

_____

Medications, Vitamins, Supplements (list what you need to have in order to take good care of yourself):

_____

_____

Now list the other non-negotiable needs and hungers that you know about. This is not a one-shot activity. As you continue to learn about yourself, you will probably discover or remember other appetites that you will add to the list. As you think about your appetites, consider the following areas of life (where we all need consistent care and feeding): relationships and support, family, intimate relationships, professional life, financial well-being, physical health and well-being, spiritual health, fun and play, learning and growth, and your physical environment (where you spend your time). Don't be afraid to list cravings or hungers that you aren't sure how to feed. If you know they are important—put them on the list!

Some possible non-negotiables to consider:

- Time outdoors
- Physical touch
- Music
- Laughter
- Spiritual time
- Stimulating conversation
- Hugs
- A sense of accomplishment
- Creative time
- Quiet time
- Time with others
- Sex
- Unplugged time (no technology)
- Being listened to
- ....

Non-negotiable needs I need to meet if I am to shine and be at my best:

_____

_____

_____

_____

What I know about myself:

Quickly, without thinking, write down as many things as you can think of that you know about yourself and your relationship with food. Be a curious data analyzer, *not* a critical judge. Make a list, write sentences or jot notes. It doesn't matter how you do it—just write what you know and don't over-think it!

Examples:

I eat at night, I like broccoli, I eat when I am stressed, I crave creamy foods, I feel out of control at buffets, I love eating break-fast, I hate my overeating, I feel most in control when I am with friends, I eat crunchy things when I am angry, I eat more when I am tired if I don't pay attention, I can eat a lot without realizing it.

I know:

_____

_____

_____

_____

_____

_____

_____

Okay. Now let's start leveraging what you *know* in ways that are helpful to you. Get curious and not judgmental. Don't think too hard before you write. Just write from your gut—and what you write doesn't have to make immediate sense to you. Don't worry about spelling or grammar or sentence structure. Focus on what you DO know, not what you don't know. Here's what you are going to write about:

What I know about how I could feed myself—my whole self, not just my stomach—better.

Don't worry about what feels do-able, just brainstorm about how you could feed yourself what you are craving:

Examples:
I could get more sleep and could work on relaxing more in the evening. I could carve out time to go for a walk every day. That would feel really good. I could set up a regular date night because my husband and I never have any time together. I could get my art supplies out and start painting again. I could make sure I take a lunch so I am not so tired and cranky in the afternoon. I could rent a funny movie on the weekends. I could leave my computer turned off on the weekends.

I know:

_____

_____

_____

_____

_____

Read over what you just wrote. Let it sink in. Now, with these ideas in mind, what are three small steps you will commit to taking **this week** to work on how you feed yourself? Think about three steps you could take that would move you closer to the action plan you have begun to create.

Examples:

I will get at least seven hours of sleep every night.

I will take time to go for a walk three days this week.

I will schedule time to have coffee with Laura on the weekend and talk about setting up regular times to get together.

Three rescue steps:

1. _____

_____

_____

2. _____

_____

_____

_____

3. _____

_____

_____

SMART TOOLS: When Self-care Seems Impossible or Makes you Squirm

Much of the time, busy women don't get what they need because they can't figure out how to make (and take) time for themselves without feeling guilty. It's impossible to prioritize yourself and your own needs if you are struggling with the belief that everyone else deserves to come ahead of you. It's impossible to fit yourself in if the time to do it never seems to exist.

This is a big problem for high-achievers who take on a great deal of responsibility, and as your success and responsibility grows, the problem usually gets worse.

If this is, in fact, a problem for you, it's going to get in the way of your attempts to make changes. It may even be causing you to have a difficult time completing the rescue plan in this book. And if *that's* the case, you may want to look at two tools that are specially designed to give you quick, do-able ways to shift your thinking so that you get better at fitting yourself in.

The How to Put Yourself First 7 Day Blast-off: This program includes 7 Days (plus some extras) of daily emails, worksheets, and short, sweet action challenges designed to help you shift your mindset and start putting yourself first. This program is entirely email-based and is delivered to your inbox daily. http://toomuchon-herplate.com/how-to-put-yourself-first/

The Success Soundtrack™ —How to Create More Ease, Joy, Me-time and Success in just 10 Minutes a Day: This audio program (mentioned previously as a mindfulness tool) consists of short, 10 minute soundtracks designed to be listened to once daily. The program also contains a (longer) bonus audio track focused on helping you identify mindset traps that can hold you back. http://toomuchonherplate.com/ successsoundtrack/

Week Two Review:

Take your time with this material; there is a lot here, and there's no need to rush through it. Remember. Stop. Breathe. Think. This is powerful stuff, and you are courageous for embarking on this program. A key component of the rescue plan is listening to yourself.

If you start to feel overwhelmed by the material, take some deep breaths and summon your curiosity. The following questions can be helpful: *What's that about? What makes me anxious/overwhelmed/angry (fill in the blank with your own word) about this?* Ask yourself if you have fallen into critical judgment mode.

Your Action Plan:

1. Work through the material at your own pace and with curiosity. You don't have to go through everything this week. You'll have next week to work on the information too.
2. Keep up with your three activities: mindfulness, journaling and the ME Log™. Remember to

plan ahead and schedule when appropriate. It's okay not to do the ME Log™ every day if it feels like too much. You can use it for a minimum of three days.

3. Answer the last three questions in this section: *What I know about myself, What I know about how I feed myself,* and *Three steps I can take.* The steps don't have to be big—in fact, you want them to be entirely do-able.

4. Be kind to yourself. This is hard work.

Ingredients for Success

"Nobody can go back and start a new beginning, but anyone can start today and make a new ending."
—MARIA ROBINSON

"If you do what you've always done, you'll get what you've always gotten."
—TONY ROBBINS

This week we will look at the process of change, sprucing up your support system, and the importance of asking for help. These are all powerful ingredients for overcoming emotional overeating.

The Rescue Plan

Read through all the material before you dive in. This week, you'll continue with **mindfulness time** for 10 minutes a day, **journaling** for 15 minutes a day, and the **ME Log™** for 3-7 days a week.

Sunday: Day 15

Take the time to schedule your journaling, your mindful activities and your ME Log™ now. Review the week ahead and decide when you will fit these activities into your schedule. Take time to review any hurdles you came up against with scheduling or with accomplishing these activities last week. Is there anything you'd like to try or do differently this week that might add more ease or help you cope more effectively with potential challenges? Note your thoughts about that here:

_____

_____

_____

_____

_____

_____

Master Schedule for Week Three

Days 15-21	Date	Mindfulness (list the mindful activity and the time you have scheduled it)	Journaling (record the time of day you will do this)	ME Log™ (check the days that you will complete)
Sunday				
Monday				
Tuesday				
Wednesday				
Thursday				
Friday				
Saturday				

Your rescue plan assignments for this week are somewhat shorter than those from last week. In addition to working on the materials for this week, you will want to review the materials from last week. Revisit questions that intrigued or stumped you. Try some of the bonus exercises. Look at the data you are collecting now and notice any shifts or changes from the previous weeks.

Monday: Day 16

You Don't Have to Do This Alone

Take a deep breath.

You have done extraordinary work. Slowing down, trying on new habits, taking a peek at behaviors you aren't particularly happy with—these things require courage.

Take a moment here to notice the thoughts and feelings you're having about your work so far. If, at this very moment, there is a judgmental part of your brain telling you all the things you *haven't* done, or all the ways you *really think you could be doing this program* "better," notice the comment, notice the judgment and then repeat after me:

> **"I am courageous."**

Because you are.

How does it feel to call yourself courageous? How can you give yourself the appropriate credit and respect for what you've taken on?

The truth is you've learned to use food in whatever way you are using it, emotional eating and all, for a reason. Looking at it from your present vantage point, it may not be the best choice for you, but, at the time when you learned to cope by using food to feed your needs and feelings, it was probably *the best solution you could envision and put into place.*

I've worked with countless emotional eaters. Not one of them woke up one morning and decided, "I'm going to choose to overeat to cope with my feelings and my needs and my life, because I know that eating this way will leave me feeling out of control and bad about myself." No one has said that. What I *do* hear a lot is, "I didn't (or don't) know what else to do—I don't know how *not* to eat emotionally."

Here is something to write on a piece of paper and post where you will see it:

"I'm doing my best."

Write that phrase down and put it where you will see it several times a day—on your desk, on your mirror, by your toothbrush. Turn on your curiosity, and observe what it feels like to say this to yourself. Can you allow it to sink in? Can you believe it? What makes it hard to accept? What if you could believe it—what would that feel like?

Try believing it for a day and see how it feels.

Write your thoughts and experiences with this here:

_____

_____

_____

_____

_____

_____

_____

Now try believing it all week.

Tuesday: Day 17

Change is a Process

Change is not a one-shot deal. Change is a process. Deciding that we are ready to *think about* making a change is as much a part of the process as the minute we actually start making the change itself.

The Emotional Eating Rescue Plan is designed to be helpful to you *wherever* you are in the process of change: contemplating it, preparing to make it, diving in to make the actual changes, or finding a way to get back on course and maintain changes you have already made. As you work through the steps of collecting data about yourself and analyzing that data, you will gain information about your readiness to move into action and make changes. Doing the work will also help you prepare to take the actions you want to take.

It can be useful to have some clarity about where you are now in relation to making active changes.

Can you identify some areas that you've studied so far where you feel ready to take action to make real concrete changes?

Remember, it's okay if you have something to write here, and it's okay if you don't. Change is a process and curiosity is what we are working with here—not self-critical judgment.

_____

_____

_____

_____

_____

Are there areas or behaviors or feelings that you are just beginning to think about and to which you might want to make changes in the future? These may be areas you want to learn more about or spend more time considering before you plan any active changes. If so, what are they? What questions or concerns do you have about making changes in these areas? What would need to happen or what would you need for you to be *more* ready to make these changes?

_____

_____

_____

_____

What about areas, behaviors or feelings that you're already addressing on which you'd like to keep working so you can continue to maintain the changes you've already made?

_____

_____

_____

_____

_____

_____

Are there feelings that come to the surface as you think and write about the possibility of change? Does it feel exciting? Scary? Overwhelming? Spend some time considering your feelings here:

_____

_____

_____

_____

_____

_____

Wednesday: Day 18

Never Underestimate the Value of Support

You do not have to do this work alone. And no one gives you extra credit for trying to. Somewhere along the line, far too many of us were taught to over-value independence, or to believe that there was something *weak* or *selfish* about asking for help or relying on others.

The truth is, *we all* need help. We function best when we have a strong support system at our disposal.

People who think big and dream big and *achieve* their dreams do so by surrounding themselves with talented people who can support their goals. Think about the most wildly successful people you know. I'm willing to bet they don't do all the work (or, as a result, attain results) in isolation.

Many people who struggle with emotional eating are uncomfortable asking for help, especially when it comes to food, eating and weight. That's the truth. Actually, many people who struggle with emotional eating are rather uncomfortable having needs or appetites to begin with. They battle that critical inner-voice that tells them they shouldn't need or want what-ever-it-is in the first place. Sound familiar?

When you live your whole life feeling uncomfortable about having needs or appetites, the logical thing to do is to distance yourself from them. That's what emotional eating often does. If you are distant from, or unable to identify what you really want or need, then, obviously, you won't be particularly good at asking for it. In fact, many times, *it won't even occur to you to ask for what you want.*

A healthy support system is an important tool in the fight against emotional eating. This week you will spend time examining the support system you currently have and identifying any changes you would like to make in that system and in how you use it.

There are two important parts to this process:

1. Identifying your support system
2. Learning to ask for the help that you need

Taking Inventory of your Support System

Let's start by talking about what support really is. A critical mistake that I see is the tendency to underestimate the benefit of high-quality support when you are putting together your emotional eating rescue plan.

Many successful women have found success by learning that they can rely on themselves. They know they're tough; in fact, many of those women feel like if they want it done "right," they need to do it themselves. While some struggle to delegate in their professional lives, they also know that success in business comes from creating and leveraging a team that can support you, expand your capabilities, and help you get where you need to go.

The place I see many smart busy women falter, is in fostering that same type of *quality* support in their personal lives. When it comes to taking control of overeating and emotional eating, too many women are making it harder than it needs to be because they believe they have to go it alone or because it feels uncomfortable to think about letting someone else in.

The truth is, nurturing a strong, active support system for yourself is one of the most effective strategies for creating changes that last. I'm not just talking about having a group of people who care about you. I'm suggesting that you evaluate your current support system in terms of its ability to *actively* help you get where you want to go.

Here's a checklist for evaluating the high-quality support you have in your life. Don't get too focused right now on what you have and what you lack. Instead, let yourself think about what it might feel like to have really great versions of each of these types of support.

High Quality Support Checklist

Who's in your corner? On whom can you rely to stand with you and support you as you strive to reach your current goals? Who are the people who want you to achieve whatever it is that *you* want to achieve?

Who holds you accountable? I'm not talking about the "diet police" here. Who is willing to hold you to your goals and your objectives in a *kind* and *helpful* way? Who helps you make sure that you follow through and asks you about it (again, in a way that feels helpful), when you haven't?

Who motivates you? On whom can you rely to remind you why you are doing the hard work involved in making changes? Who can you count on to hold up that picture of your final destination and encourage you to keep going? Who reminds you how far you've come and all the ways your efforts will or are paying off?

Who do you celebrate with when you achieve victories along the way? Acknowledging the milestones on the way to the finish line is exceedingly important in maintaining motivation and feeling good about the work you're doing. Who encourages you to celebrate when you decide you are "too busy" to revel in your success?

Who believes in you? Who are the people in your support system who know you're capable of achieving what you set out to achieve? These are the ones who can tell you *why* you're able to be successful. They know your strengths and help you see how you can leverage them to move forward more easily. They remind you of your enormous capacity for success during the times when you might not believe that you can accomplish a particular goal.

Who is your example? Are you the leader of the pack—the one who motivates everyone else—or do you have someone in your support system who is one or two steps ahead of you? Are you reinventing the wheel or learning from the wisdom of others who have succeeded before you? We tend to see more possibilities and grow more when we're surrounded by others who encourage us to stretch our ideas of what we believe we can do.

Who is your sounding board? With whom do you talk things through? To whom do you turn to brainstorm strategies, tweak plans that aren't working for you, get advice or just blow off steam after a tough day?

Who tells you the hard truth? Who do you trust to tell you (in a supportive and helpful way) when you are missing the boat or getting in your own way? Sometimes strong women send out the vibe that they're "fine," they "have it under control," and they don't need help. The truth is, we all need help sometimes. Who are the people who will take you to task when you aren't taking care of yourself or are trying to gut it out on your own and it isn't working?

Use these questions to identify any holes in your support network. Doing so will pay off.

Your support system

Let's take a look at the support system that you have in place and on which you currently rely. These are the people with whom you feel safe and who support you in meeting your goals. Each individual (or group) probably plays a unique role in your support system, helping you in various ways and different areas of your life.

List the people or groups that can support you in some way as you work on changing your relationship with food and with eating. Examples might be *my best friend, my walking group, my physician, the women I eat lunch with at work.* Don't worry or judge yourself if you have a hard time with this. Most people will find they could benefit from expanding their support system:

_____

_____

_____

_____

_____

_____

Are there sources of support that are available to you that you *don't* utilize? A trap that busy women can easily fall into is the mindset of "I'm-too-busy-to-explain-this-to-someone-else." Do you find yourself thinking it's just faster to do it yourself but then feel like you are responsible for just about everything? If so, it's important to begin taking a longer range perspective. Do you cling to the notion that you "shouldn't need to ask for help"? Judging your needs this way can create huge barriers to creating both more ease *and* more success in your life.

Here are some additional questions to consider about building a strong and effective support system. Are their connections with others that you'd like to make stronger? Would you like more personal support, or would you love to work with a coach, join a program, or find a support group? Are you looking for a kind of support that you don't know how to find?

The first step to creating your ideal support system is drawing a clear picture of what you want.

Spend some time thinking about and then describing how you would like your support system to be different, stronger, bigger or more effective. Don't worry about being *reasonable* or *realistic* or even about how you will make this happen. Allow yourself to dream about what you really want. What kinds of support are you craving?

_____

_____

_____

_____

_____

_____

Do you have any ideas about how you might create or find some of the support you just described? Any ideas of places with which you might connect or investigate that could move your support system one small degree closer to your vision? Remember to think beyond individual contacts. In addition to friendships and family relationships, consider possible groups that might be supportive, on-line message boards or forums, mentors, and other professional sources of help and support.

Write any ideas you have for building your support system here:

_____

_____

_____

_____

_____

_____

Are there barriers or obstacles that seem to prevent you from getting the support you need? If so, list them, describe them and say anything you need to about them here. Make sure to note any judgments or self-critical ideas that might get in the way of seeking support for yourself. Remember, for many high-achievers, one of the biggest barriers to getting quality support is the false belief that you *shouldn't need help* or that you are somehow stronger if you go it alone. Is this a mindset that is holding you back? What might you gain if you could step beyond this notion?

_____

_____

_____

_____

_____

It can be tempting to withdraw from people when you need them the most. If you've been feeling disappointed in yourself or overly frustrated with your eating, it's a good time to ask yourself whether you have pulled back from people who have been a part of your support system in the past. It can be helpful to make some deliberate and small steps to reconnect or to stay connected to the people we care about during challenging times. This might mean setting a goal of calling a friend daily, or posting on a message board each morning.

Are there specific goals for maintaining or building support that might be helpful to you? If you are ready to set some goals and you think it would be helpful, write them here:

_____

_____

_____

_____

_____

_____

_____

Thursday: Day 19

Asking for Help

Successful people are good at asking themselves what they need. People stuck in self-critical judgment are good at telling themselves they shouldn't need *anything*.

Feeling uncomfortable about asking for help is a key factor to remaining stuck.

We become skilled at ignoring or covering up our feelings when we don't know what else to do about them. Some of us developed emotional eating habits because we didn't know what else to do with overwhelming feelings or our reactions to overwhelming experiences—so we ate. Using the tools in this program will help you grow more aware of your feelings, needs and desires. Learning to ask for help is a powerful strategy for coping with many of these needs and feelings and appetites.

Quite often, clients will tell me, "I felt anxious (or bored or lonely or angry or some other painful feeling) and I didn't know what else to do, so I ate."

A powerful change you can make is to transform the situation "I didn't know what else to do" from a cue *to eat* into a cue to *reach out to your support system.*

Asking for help will mean vastly different things to different people. It may mean asking for support or asking to be heard. It may mean asking for help brainstorming a solution. It might be asking for something concrete such as help making dinner or help with a problem. It might mean feeling comfortable enough to *ask for the time* to take better care of yourself or do something that is important to you.

Letting Help In

If it's hard for you to ask for help, try this:

Spend a day noticing the things for which you *don't* ask for help. Be curious about any patterns that you observe. Did you think about asking for help and decide not to? Did you realize that you could have asked for help after the fact? What led to your remaining silent when you really wanted and needed to ask for help? Write about your thoughts and experiences here:

_____

_____

_____

_____

List as many things as you can think of with which you'd like to have help (dare to dream here!). Feel free to list concrete things such as mowing the lawn and less tangible things like "I'd like someone to help me stay motivated with my weight loss goals." Don't worry about whether you'd feel you could ask for these things today, and don't worry about *how* someone could possibly help you—just write down the areas with which you'd like to have help.

_____

_____

_____

_____

_____

_____

Friday and Saturday: Days 20 & 21

Practice Asking for Help

Set a goal to ask for help five times each day. Yes—five times. You don't have to ask for big things, but give yourself an opportunity to warm up your "asking" muscles.

Here are some questions to ponder after you've done your asking. What was it like to do it? What was difficult about it? Did anything surprise you when you asked for help? What kind of results (help) did you receive (or not receive)?

_____

_____

_____

_____

_____

_____

Keep this in mind: Asking for help is a sign of strength. It is one of the most important ways that we take care of ourselves, and it takes courage.

Week Three Review:

Take a deep breath and ask yourself how it's going. In just three weeks, you have covered a lot of ground, and much of it may be new and unfamiliar. Remember that change is not a one shot deal. You can review this material more than once—and you'll want to. Each time you do, you're likely to take something new from it.

How are you doing with staying curious? Are you growing more aware of the times you fall into self-critical judgment? Have you developed any tools for pulling yourself out of criticism and getting curious again? Who do you know who might help you? Alternately, do you know other people who also struggle with emotional eating? Might you be able to help each other?

Busy Women's Tip: The Quick & Easy Way to Ask for Help

Have you ever found yourself in a place where it feels like you simply don't have time to ask for help? You know, the "it's faster to do it myself" place or the "I don't even know how to explain it" place?

If you're busy or overwhelmed, it might feel like too much work even to *think* about asking for help. And that's another one of those mind traps that can leave you feeling stuck, frustrated, or like you just want to stop thinking about all of it and go get the mint chocolate chip ice cream from the freezer.

Here's a tip: Asking for help can be easier if you don't put so much pressure on yourself.

When you're asking for help, sometimes all you need to know is that you need it. One place smart cookies get stuck is when they tell themselves they can't ask for help because they "don't even know what to ask for."

Next time you are hoping someone can help you, try explaining the situation instead of the solution. Tell them what's going on and then say, "Is there a way you could help me with this?" or "How do you think you could help?" or an open-ended "Do you think you could help me?" When you're feeling stumped and see no solution in sight, it's a perfect opportunity to say, "I don't know what to do here. Can you help?"

SMART TOOLS: Places to get more help

Emotional Eating Coaching

The program in this book is an outgrowth of the personal coaching programs and retreats that I run with women worldwide. In those relationships, I work with my clients to target their specific problems and goals, identify their unique strengths and talents and help them to strategize around roadblocks, crafting their individual paths to success.

Working with a coach can be a powerful addition to your support system. A coach is someone you select as your partner to help you meet your goals, set your plan in motion, maintain motivation, stay accountable, and continue moving in the direction you want to go.

The Emotional Eating Rescue Plan for Smart, Busy Women is designed so that you can work through the material on your own, in your own way and at your own pace, but some people will find they want additional help and support.

You can learn more about private coaching and current events and programs at the Too Much on Her Plate website: http://TooMuchonHerPlate.com.

When to talk with a therapist

Therapy, like coaching, is a powerful tool. If the hurt you have is really big, and if feeling your feelings means you are being pulled back into past experiences and situations that aren't resolved in your mind, you might benefit from help in sorting them out.

Therapists are experts in helping people untangle the past so that they can move forward. If your feelings about an experience from the past become overwhelming when you try to examine them, if you feel plagued by feelings such as sadness or fear or anger that don't pass, if you're unable to sleep or feel depressed or anxious, and the feelings aren't changing or passing, or if you are having thoughts about or impulses toward self-harm, then seeking a skilled therapist can be an extremely helpful and important thing to do. If you are suffering from an eating disorder such as anorexia nervosa or bulimia nervosa, you should seek treatment from a qualified mental health professional who specializes in the treatment of eating disorders. You can obtain a referral for a psychologist who works with emotional eating issues by contacting the Psychological Association in your state, province or community.

Your Action Plan:

1. Continue working through the material from last week on "analyzing your data." Remember to approach the questions at your own pace and with curiosity. Note any places where you "get stuck" and move on. Allow the questions that stump you to percolate in your brain, and be aware of what comes up.

2. Keep up with your three activities: mindfulness, journaling and the ME Log™. Remember to plan ahead and schedule when appropriate. It's

okay not to do the ME Log™ every day if it feels like too much. If that's the case, cut back to three days (and don't forget to ask yourself *why* it was feeling like too much).

3. Read and work through the items and rescue plan activities in this section.

4. What is the next step to take toward feeding yourself and your spirit in the best possible way? Choose something that feels do-able and that you will commit to accomplishing *this week*. When you write it down, remember to be concrete about *what* you will do and *when* you will do it.

In the next seven days I will commit to:

_____

_____

_____

_____

_____

_____

5. Remember, there is strength in numbers. Practice letting more support into your life.

Setting Your GPS

"If you don't know where you are going, you'll end up someplace else."

—Yogi Berra

"A year from now you may wish you had started today."

—Karen Lamb

The Rescue Plan

This is the last week of the four week Rescue Plan, but that doesn't mean that you should necessarily be almost finished with this book. The rescue plan is designed to be recycled, reworked, rehashed and relearned—for as long as you want.

I encourage you to wear out your copy of this book. Each time you review these questions and activities, you'll learn something new. Because you are always applying your own data—and that data is ever-changing, the material will continue to evolve with you. In fact, one of my favorite goals set by a participant in her fourth week of this program was to start the program all over and do it again—because she saw that she was now in a totally different place from when she first started, and she knew that going through the materials a second time would lead her to a different (and deeper) place.

The final part of your rescue plan focuses on fine tuning your internal GPS so your goals will keep moving you forward and provide a clear map of where you want to go. I've also included some important information about getting stuck which, incidentally, happens to all of us and is part of the journey.

Sunday: Day 22

Take the time to schedule your journaling, your mindful activities and your ME Log™ now. Review the week ahead and decide when you will fit these activities into your schedule. If you want, go back and review or work on any incomplete activities from the previous two weeks.

Take time to review any hurdles you faced with scheduling or with moving forward with the rescue plan last week. How can you make adjustments this week? Write any notes or thoughts about that here:

_____

_____

_____

_____

Master Schedule for Week Four

Days 22-28	Date	Mindfulness (list the mindful activity and the time you have scheduled it)	Journaling (record the time of day you will do this)	ME Log™ (check the days that you will complete)
Sunday				
Monday				
Tuesday				
Wednesday				
Thursday				
Friday				
Saturday				

Monday: Day 23

Staying on Course

Years ago, when my husband and I decided to buy our first house, our realtor asked us to begin by making a list of everything we wanted and dreamed of in a home. She wanted us to draw the most accurate map we could of the place that we were looking for. She didn't know if our dream home existed, or if we could afford it, but she knew that if we didn't clearly state what we wanted, we were a lot less likely to find it.

Make sure you have a map

If you don't create a clear agenda, you may not get where you want to go.

That sounds pretty obvious. And yet, we can easily become disconnected from our goals and priorities. We often feel too busy to think outside our day-to-day lives, and we're constantly surrounded by messages about what we should want, what we need to buy, what we should be hungry for, and even what we should aspire to look like. It's easy to be swept away by the priorities the media, our bosses, our partners, and our families have for us.

The decision to complete this rescue plan was a major commitment that you made to yourself. You have invested your time, your energy, and most importantly, your *hope* in creating a relationship with food that works better for you than it has in the past and that will help you achieve your goals. Even so, with all that you've given, it can still be a struggle to honor your goals as a priority. I want to challenge you to do it anyway. Because creating the success you hunger for is going to require keeping your eye on the prize and keeping yourself on your priority list.

Getting off track

When we *don't* take the time to define what we truly want—our goals, priorities, and needs—it is much too easy to get wrapped up in living life based on the priorities of others. When we *don't* take the time to draw a map and chart a course for where we want to go, we often get "too busy" and end up using all our time completing the tasks on our "to-do" lists.

Before we know it, it's the end of the day or the month or the year, and we just "didn't get to" the promises we made to ourselves.

When we fall into this pattern, we end up chasing our lives rather than intentionally creating them. It's an easy trap in which to get stuck. It's also an easy trap to rationalize—"I guess this is just how life has to be right now." Not true.

Purposeful living is living with *deliberate purpose*, moving on a path of our own creation. Reactive living is the opposite; it's life on the defensive.

Living reactively means not being in charge of the path you are on. Feeling out of control, stressed out, overwhelmed or trapped are all major clues that your life is out of balance and that you are in the position of *reacting* to your life. These feelings are also major triggers for emotional eating.

We're all busy, and we all spend time doing things we don't really want to do, or responding to someone else's idea of what is important at the moment. If there is not a strong thread of intention, however, a sense of purpose, woven throughout our lives, if the reacting starts to take the bulk of our energy, then life begins to feel like a hamster wheel moving at an out-of-control speed—and even though we're moving fast, we won't get where we want to go.

Is life leading you or are you leading your life?

How can you identify a life that's off track? It's when the three things you would list as most important to you are the last things that receive your attention—or when you don't even know what those three things are. It's when you are so focused on "getting everything done" that you are eating too much (or too little), or eating the wrong food, not spending time with the people you care about, drinking too much alcohol or caffeine, watching too much TV, not getting outside or getting the exercise you really need for your health—not being the person that you want to be with and for yourself and others.

It's important to clarify—living with purpose is about working *toward* getting life the way you want it. It is a *process*, not the final destination. Moving intentionally through life can be achieved in very small steps, even in the midst of busy, demanding lives.

Here are steps for identifying your priorities and goals and for making sure that the life map you're using will take you where you want to go.

What are the three most important things in your life?

1. _____

2. _____

3. _____

How much quality time did you spend on each of these three things in the last week? Was it enough?

Stating our priorities is one thing. The way we live and expend our life energy tells the truth about the priorities we are actually living.

Post your three top priorities somewhere where you will see them often—by your computer, your refrigerator, on your phone.

Are your values and actions in alignment? If not, I challenge you to come up with one small way you can begin to make a shift.

My life would be more in alignment with my priorities if I:

Examples:

> *"My life would be more in alignment with my priorities if I kept my commitment to attend my yoga class instead of cancelling to work late."*

> *"My life would be more in alignment with my priorities if I allowed myself to sit down and eat a dinner that I enjoy—on a plate—in the evenings."*

> *"My life would be more in alignment with my priorities if I said "no" to some of the obligations that are causing me stress so I could spend more time with my family and with friends."*

———————————————————————

———————————————————————

———————————————————————

———————————————————————

———————————————————————

———————————————————————

Where do you want to go?

You've been curious about a lot in your life over the last three weeks, and it's important to know that it's not humanly possible to have digested and metabolized all the thinking and the work you've done by now.

What you've experienced is an *introduction*. I've shown you some key strategies and tools for getting to the bottom of your emotional eating and for helping you to identify patterns, issues and "stuck" spots that you might have with your eating and your weight loss.

You've had time to play around with these tools and practice implementing them in your own life. Practice doesn't mean "perfect," and you may not yet have found how best to use the tools for yourself. For many people, that takes time and that's okay. You probably haven't answered all the questions in this book to your satisfaction and if you have, I urge you to ask them a few more times.

Absorbing the material and thinking about these areas of your life is a *process*, not a single act.

For many people, the first step in practicing with the tools is finding out what *doesn't* work. Having experiences where you *don't* feel satisfied with how you are using the tools, and where struggling to use the tools as instruments of curiosity and not judgment are valuable learning experiences.

When you first try out the tools in the rescue plan, some of you will meet your defenses head on. That's okay. That's how you get to know them better. It's really only when we befriend our resistance and our fears that we can learn to move beyond them in an *enduring* or lasting way.

The goal at the end of four weeks is *not* to be "done."

In fact, life seldom works that way. The goal at the end of this rescue plan is to know what the tools are, to have begun to develop some ideas about how they work best for you, to have learned some things about being curious, and through that, about your relationship with food. And to know what *your* next steps are.

Steps are different from leaps. It's easy to get stuck in judging the size of your steps. But steps of any size are what get us where we want to go. Remember that this process is more like a marathon—an endurance event—than a sprint.

Tuesday: Day 24

The Next Steps

Think about your health, wellness and life goals, both in the bigger and the more immediate picture.

I'm going to ask you to create three sets of goals: 30-day goals, 90-day goals and one-year goals. I'd like you to set three of each and write them down. Your goals may be related or build on each other. For instance, a 30-day goal may be a stepping stone to your one-year goal, or they may be distinct and unconnected.

I want you to focus on what are known as S.M.A.R.T. goals, goals that meet the following criteria: *S*pecific, *Mea*surable, *A*ttainable, *R*ealistic and *T*ime-bound[2].

Wanting to get in shape is not a S.M.A.R.T. goal. Being able to do 10 push ups or walk five miles by a specific deadline meets the guidelines. Losing 50 pounds is a specific goal, but, depending on the deadline you've set for yourself, it may or may not meet the "realistic" criterion.

Give yourself some time to think about and consider your goals. Do some journaling or go for a mindful walk and mull over what *you know* about what you want to do next. When you're ready, record your goals here:

30-Day Goals

1. _____

_____

_____

_____

2 The SMART acronym first appeared in the November 1981 issue of Management Review. It was referred to by its creator George T. Doran in his article, "There's a S.M.A.R.T. way to write management goals and objectives."

Doran, G. T. (1981). There's a S.M.A.R.T. way to write management's goals and objectives. Management Review, Volume 70, Issue 11(AMA FORUM), pp. 35–36.

2. _____

_____

_____

3. _____

_____

_____

90-Day Goals

1. _____

_____

_____

2. _____

_____

_____

3. _____

_____

One Year Goals

1. _____

_____

_____

2. _____

_____

_____

3. _____

_____

_____

If you aren't already setting clear goals in your life, you may be surprised by the momentum that can be created simply by stating what you want. Review and update your goals at least every three months. Keep a current list someplace where you will see it frequently.

The single act of defining your intentions is a powerful one. It is the preliminary and necessary step for defining the life you want to live and setting your course.

Wednesday: Day 25

Make It Bold, Juicy, and Inspiring

Today's step is to begin to take a closer look at your vision for your future. We'll start with the 30-Day Goals you designed. Pick one 30-Day Goal. Review it carefully and make sure that it's really a SMART goal—Specific, Measurable, Attainable, Realistic and Time-bound. If your goal doesn't meet all the criteria, reword it or redesign it so that it does.

Now step back and squint at it. We want to make sure this is a compelling 30-Day Goal for you. Make sure it's something that you *really* want. Don't pick goals that seem dull or boring or that feel like someone else's "should." A "should" goal is something like *I should lose weight* or *I should lower my cholesterol.* It might be important, but it doesn't give you a happy feeling in your stomach when you think about accomplishing it.

If you are stuck with a "should" goal or a list of goals that make you tired just thinking about them or ones that don't light you up or make you smile, go back to your drawing board and work on making your goal into something that's bold and juicy.

One technique for creating bold, juicy, compelling goals (my favorite kind) is to keep digging through the dull goals until you find them. You can do this using curiosity. Yep—curiosity is the duct tape in your rescue plan. It's good for just about everything, and it has great potential to help you here too.

Let's say you have a goal that bores you to tears like *"I should lose 45 pounds."* Apply curiosity to that goal by asking "Why is this something I want to do?"

Here's an example from a client we'll call Amber. She's a client who really did want to lose 45 pounds and really was bored to tears and pretty uninspired by her goal and the big undertaking she saw ahead. In fact, when she first told me about the weight she wanted to lose, she might have easily been describing signing up for a root canal. Here's the conversation we had as we drilled down (speaking of root canal!) to a more motivating goal.

M: Why do you want to lose weight?

A: Because I'm not healthy at this weight.

M: Why do you want to be healthy?

A: Because my knees hurt, and it's not as easy to move as it used to be.

M: Why do you want to be more agile and have less pain?

A: Because I can't do a lot of things I used to do anymore. It hurts to ballroom dance—I used to compete and dance every weekend. I miss dancing and the time with my friends who would go with me. I miss how it felt to move effortlessly across the floor.

As we talked more about dancing, Amber teared up as she decribed her love for it and the fun she used to have. Her energy changed, and she became more animated as she talked about how it felt to glide on the dance floor, and to be doing something that came so easily to her. Getting back to fun and pain-free, joy-filled ballroom dancing was Amber's bold juicy goal, and getting there was going to include taking control of her eating and her weight so that she could make it happen.

Once we pushed passed Amber's uninspiring "should" goal, she quickly moved from feeling irritated to inspired, motivated, and even excited.

Not only did Amber now have her GPS dialed in to a clear goal that inspired her and that she *really* wanted to achieve, she also had a vivid picture of what success would look and feel like for her. Her vision went from seeing an arbitrary number on a scale to envisioning herself swirling on the dance floor in a new red dress, laughing with her friends, and feeling like she had her mojo back.

Can *you* feel the difference? Amber certainly did.

Try the *why* questioning with your goal. You may find that even a pretty juicy goal can be more endearing or exciting than you originally thought.

If you now have new or upgraded, juicier goals, list them below.

30-Day Goals

1. _____

_____

_____

_____

2. _____

_____

_____

3. _____

_____

_____

90-Day Goals

1. _____

_____

_____

2. _____

_____

_____

3. _____

_____

_____

One Year Goals

1. _____

_____

2. _____

_____

3. _____

_____

_____

Okay, *now* let's start making your 30-day goals into realities. Pick one 30-Day Bold, Juicy and Inspiring Goal. Begin with the one that feels the most interesting and most compelling.

What are the first three reasonable (not too big and not too small) steps toward achieving this goal? Hint: think about steps that would bump you one inch closer, not propel you all the way there.

Design three steps that you can take this week. Make sure they are possible. Create a clear picture of you taking these steps. Include every detail—the *when*, the *where*, the *how*.

Goal:

_____

_____

_____

Three steps:

1. _____

_____

_____

2. _____

_____

_____

3. _____

_____

_____

_____

If you are ready, take a deep breath and commit to these steps. Schedule them and put them on your calendar.

If you aren't feeling ready, allow yourself to be curious and ask yourself "why?"

It may be counterintuitive, but it's important *not* to get into the judgmental mindset that you *should* be ready. Instead, try to understand *why* you are feeling resistance. Does the goal need tweaking? Is it too ambitious? Are the steps not right for you? Are you afraid? If the steps are scary or anxiety-provoking, can you slow them down or make them smaller?

Goal setting and designing the steps to achieve your goal can be tricky because we often misjudge the size of what's possible. Most of us tend to overestimate what we can do in a month and underestimate what we can do in a year. Take a look at your goal and the steps you see toward it, and make sure everything is the right size for the time you have to spend on it.

One more thing—don't forget all that good stuff we covered about support. If you feel anxious about moving forward, you might be craving more help. It's almost always worth looking at whether you can increase the support or help you have in reaching your goal.

Keep questioning and tweaking until you feel committed and on board with your plan and your action steps.

Thursday: Day 26

Choose another 30-Day Goal, make sure it's compelling, juicy, and truly *yours* and then follow the same steps you followed yesterday.

Goal:

_____

_____

_____

Three steps:

1. _____

_____

2. _____

_____

3. _____

_____

Friday: Day 27

Take your final Bold, Juicy 30-Day Goal and follow the same steps you followed the last two days.

Busy Women's Tip:

Five Things to Consider When You Just Can't Get Your Butt in Gear

We've all been there. You have goals—important ones— and maybe even a plan that seems do-able. And yet, when push comes to shove, you just can't get your butt in gear. What's that about?

The truth is, many smart, busy women struggle when it comes to figuring out how to take better care of themselves or how to focus their time and energy on something that's important to them.

If you're wondering where your mojo went or why you just can't seem to prioritize your goals and make them happen, ask yourself these five important questions. They may just help you figure out what's holding you back:

1. **Do you need more motivation?** If you aren't getting where you want to go, it's important to ask whether you want it badly enough. Making lifestyle changes is hard, and if you're doing something just because you "should" or to make someone else happy, your motivation, passion, and drive are going to falter (if not fizzle out all-together). We make changes (and stick to them) when we have a workable plan *and* a compelling enough reason or a juicy enough reward *to stick with it*. If you are stuck or feel like you are moving in circles, ask yourself what's motivating you these days? What's the incentive? When do you get to celebrate and reap the rewards? Sprinkle these

in liberally—even daily—so you'll have frequent reminders that what you are doing is paying off.

2. **Do you have enough energy?** Do you have enough energy to pursue this goal? Are you being realistic about what you can do, and are you well-rested enough to achieve it? Many of my clients (busy women with a lot on their plates), not only expect a *lot* (often too much) of themselves, they also expect to be able to function with less than everyone else. Big mistake. For 99.9% of us, long term success will not happen on five hours of sleep a night. Make the first step toward getting your butt in gear the step of consistently getting 7.5 hours of sleep a night. Your productivity, your creativity, your focus, and even your metabolism will thank you. This is one mojo-enhancing step where the payoff is HUGE.

3. **Have you said no so you can say yes?** Just because you want to do it doesn't mean you can stretch time to fit it in. Every yes requires a no in order to make space for it. If you are wilting instead of thriving in terms of your goals, ask yourself whether there is room in your life to move forward. What are you willing to say no to so that you can block out the time and the energy that you need to create success? Consider your success an extraordinarily valuable investment. Just as you save money for big purchases like a car or a house, you need to save and preserve your time and energy (and yes, sometimes your dollars), so that you have them to invest in the valuable results you seek.

4. **What soundtrack are you listening to?** One of the biggest drains on your energy, your mojo, and your motivation can be the way you think and talk to yourself. Perfectionism, self-blame, frustration and anger can all sabotage your ability to start and stick with the changes you are trying to make. Are you too hard on yourself? Do you struggle to put yourself first or flounder with the idea of how to prioritize your needs? My litmus test is pretty simple. Would you talk to your mother the way you judge and talk to yourself? Do you *believe* in your ability to be successful? If your mindset and self-talk are getting in your way, don't despair—but don't ignore them either. Focus on practices that build confidence and effectiveness and eradicate beliefs that limit success.

5. **Who can help?** There are few things more discouraging than feeling stuck or ineffective. The payoff for moving beyond this is huge. Consider how you feel when you achieve or win or cross whatever finish line you've set for yourself. If you aren't making progress, can't get motivated or aren't seeing the results you want, consider whether some assistance, instruction, mentoring or coaching is in order. Do you need more tools, a fresh perspective, or a shoulder to lean on? Remember that one of the most self-sabotaging mindsets, particularly for hard-working high-achievers, is the belief that "I should be able to figure this out on my own." Use your newly honed "asking for help" skills to get what you need so that you can get moving again.

Goal:

_____

_____

_____

Three steps:

1. _____

_____

2. _____

_____

3. _____

_____

Saturday: Day 28

A Note about Getting Stuck

Momentum and action are great, but they aren't all there is when it comes to making changes. Change is a process, not one distinct action. And stumbling is a part of it.

You know how it plays out when change *doesn't* work: you dive into it bright-eyed and bushy tailed. For the first few days (or even weeks) you're on fire. You're making progress and feeling good about it. But after a while it's not so fun, or you're not so prepared, or you're tired...

This is the time when people who don't have good built-in accountability and support might find their resolve fading and their goals and plans starting to disappear from the top of their priority list as they quietly feel discouraged—again.

What's going on? They've hit a slump.

Slumps have gotten a very bad rap. The slump is not the problem. It's what we do with them.

Without the right perspective, people in a slump can cause themselves a lot of pain.

They tend to feel guilty. They beat themselves up because they don't feel successful. Instead, they feel ashamed for being "weak" or "lazy." Shame silences people and compels them to pull back and hide their struggling. People stuck in slumps tend not to ask for help. They often come to the conclusion that they have failed again and that they are never going to meet their goal.

Slumps are totally misunderstood

As an expert in helping people make changes, I love slumps. Slumps can be some of the most powerful moments in the process of change. A good slump can get you on the road to creating lasting success like nothing else.

Here's what I mean. *A slump does not mean you have failed. A slump simply indicates a lack of alignment between you and your plan.*

If you can be *curious* about the slump instead of judgmental, you can gather valuable information. Assuming you still believe your goal is a good one, *this* is the place where you can really make progress.

The number one mistake that people make when they hit a slump is believing that they have failed.

If you find yourself in this spot—here's the important truth. *You* didn't fail. Your *plan* did. And if you're like most of us, you may have hit this slump or roadblock in the past (that's why it feels particularly discouraging).

This is the place for some curious, *nonjudgmental* self-evaluation and plan tweaking. Where did you get hung up? What didn't go as planned? What was the tough spot you couldn't surmount? How could making the change have been easier?

In other words, how did your plan fail you?

Successful change almost never occurs in a straight line

Change tends to happen in an upward moving spiral. We circle through our old mistakes, but we continue to move upward in the direction we want to go. The difference between going in circles and moving up a spiral is that, in a spiral, you have more knowledge and more coping tools at each go-round. And each revolution brings you further along in your progress.

If you can ditch the self-blame and summon curiosity instead, you'll likely come up with some information that will help you revamp your plan and keep moving up the spiral. If you don't, however, don't be tempted to slink back into your cave of shame.

This is exactly the time and place to reach out and ask for help. There are other people who have either a) figured this stuff out already, or b) know a lot about change and can help you navigate this bumpy blip on your spiral so you can start circling upward again.

My client Lena told me that she simply could not stick with her plans for healthy eating and exercise. She was extremely frustrated with the pattern she described of getting started, beginning to lose weight and be more active, and then feeling like it all fell apart. She felt like she lacked discipline and willpower. She believed that if she could stick with the new emotional eating tools she was learning, things could change, but she couldn't maintain any of the routines she was developing and felt like she could never develop the momentum or the habits that she needed. Did I mention she was really mad at herself about all this?

Lena was SO frustrated with herself that she wasn't able to see the bigger picture. When I encouraged her to step back and look at her situation with compassion and curiosity, an important pattern emerged. Lena is a partner in a business which requires her to travel frequently and sometimes unpredictably. Every time she started to develop a routine with her emotional eating tools, taking time for herself, and exercise, the need to travel would throw her off track. When she was on the road, she didn't have the same schedule or structure that she was relying on to maintain her new habits. To add to the problem, returning from her trips was also quite stressful. Often she came back (with jet lag) to a long list of chores and responsibilities—and to an empty refrigerator. Lena didn't need more willpower. What she needed was a plan that fit the demands of her life.

Where are you moving through a spiral and where are you going in circles? What's working? What isn't? What could *you* fine-tune?

Places in my life, issues or relationships where I tend to get stuck:

_____

_____

_____

_____

_____

_____

What could you do differently? Do you need to schedule your personal priorities the way you schedule your professional ones (or your children's)? Do you need more built-in rewards, or would creating additional support or accountability keep you on target? Could you find someone to help you get or stay on track?

When Lena was able to step out of her self-blame, it was very clear that she needed a plan for staying on track when she was traveling. At first she insisted that this was simply impossible, but I encouraged her to stay curious and focus on small changes that felt do-able. She decided to set better boundaries on her work day when she traveled and set aside specific time in the morning to focus on her own needs. Lena came up with a strategy that allowed her to use the ME Log™ in restaurants without feeling self-conscious. She also asked her assistant to book hotel rooms that had a fitness center she could use. The change that Lena felt most proud of was putting a plan in place to make her homecoming easier. She committed to asking for more help from her family and now often texts them a grocery or to-do list before she returns so that she comes home to fresh produce and less stress.

Do some brainstorming. What could help you do it differently—*not* get stuck, or get "unstuck" the next time you end up dealing with your challenging situations? Write about any ideas you have here. Don't worry if you don't have a "perfect" or complete solution. Just brainstorm and write down any ideas that come to mind.

_____

_____

_____

_____

_____

_____

What small changes could you make that might help the gears of your life and your plans turn more easily? For instance, many of my clients find that having a "no brainer" back up idea for a healthy meal (one they can easily pull out of the freezer or grab-and-go in some way) helps them stay on track when life gets crazy. Most find it essential to have some well-planned strategies *before* they travel. On a daily basis, it may be useful to think about whether there are stressful or even mundane activities that you could delegate or decline so that you have more time to focus on your priorities. Simple changes like having someone else help with grocery shopping or errands or not checking your email in the evening can help reduce overload and stress and make life work better.

When you review your own life, what small changes would you like to consider? Note any ideas here:

_____

_____

_____

_____

_____

_____

_____

_____

Week Four Review:

It's fitting to end this four-week program where we began—with the ground rules. Here they are again:

The Rules that Lead to Rescue

These are the underpinnings of the program. When all else fails, when you feel like you are lost or stuck, come back to these four principles. If you take nothing else from this program, take these. Write them down in a place where you will see them often. They are what you need to get back on track and keep moving forward.

1. Knowledge is power—never forget that you have a lot of knowledge. Above all, and when all else "fails," be curious. Ask yourself *what can I learn from this?*
2. Follow the SCUBA training guidelines: Stop, Breathe, Think and Act.
3. You overeat for a reason. Always. Never ignore your hunger. Identify it, respect it, and make every effort to feed yourself in the highest quality, most appropriate way.
4. Remember that change is not a one shot deal and that the process of change is seldom a straight, smooth line. It's normal to have a bumpy path with plateaus and stuck spots along the way. Usually we need to learn a lesson more (sometimes a lot more) than once.

Your Action Plan:

1. Take the time to think about and develop short and longer-term goals for yourself. Write them down and review them every few months.

2. Give yourself permission to approach these changes as a process—not an-all-or-nothing-one-time thing.

3. Review the *Emotional Eating Rescue Plan* ground rules. If you haven't already done so, print them out and put them some place where you'll see them frequently and be reminded of them.

4. Continue to take the time to schedule the tools—the journaling, the mindfulness and the ME Log™. Continue the ways and the style of using them that is useful to you.

What Comes After the Rescue?

At this point, after 28 days of curious exploration, you may be feeling an interesting mix of relief and upheaval as you continue to sift through new perspectives and strategies. I'll admit it can be both soothing and unsettling to move through all the places in your mind and spirit that you've visited over the past four weeks. Be sure to give yourself some time (and patience and compassion) to digest and metabolize it all. It's an important part of the process.

Sometimes I get my best ideas in the shower or on a run, and I believe it's at those times because that's when the pressure is off, my mind has a chance to relax, to sift through what it knows, and to make sense of it all. That's when the "aha" moments and the creativity can really surge. The same thing may happen for you.

So be gentle with yourself if you are experiencing some confusion or feeling a bit overloaded. It's all part of making peace with food and with your life.

I'd love to hear where your rescue plan takes you, so please do stay in touch if it suits you. Here are some ways to connect, to get ongoing tips, information and resources, and to be the first to know about upcoming programs or events:

http://TooMuchonHerPlate.com: Go here to subscribe to receive timely updates and articles. You can also sign up for my free audio series: *5 Simple Steps to Move Beyond Overwhelm with Food and Life.*

Connect on Facebook:
http://Facebook.com/TooMuchonHerPlate

Connect on Twitter:
http://Twitter.com/MelissaMcCreery

Whatever your next step is from here, I wish you much success and I wish you well.

Take good care,
Melissa

SMART TOOLS

One of my favorite philosophers and self-help authors is actually Dr. Seuss. Under that pen name, Theodor S. Geisel and his wife Audrey S. Geisel wrote a great book called *Oh, the Places You'll Go*. The Library of Congress description calls it "Advice in rhyme for proceeding in life; weathering fear, loneliness, and confusion; and being in charge of your actions." I love that description.

If you haven't already read it, find a copy because the advice is superb. It will make you smile, and it would be an excellent and gentle companion as you move through whatever next steps you have chosen.

I'm on the same page with Dr. Seuss. Getting where we are going is not always simple, mistakes *will* get made. We will try and we will goof up, and then we will keep on trying. And with patience, we can figure it out and we can get there. Every time I read *Oh, the Places You'll Go*, I am reminded that my struggles are simply human struggles, that there is a light at the end of the tunnel, and that it's all good.

> "You're off to Great Places!
> Today is your day!
> Your mountain is waiting,
> So...get on your way!"

> —Dr. Seuss, *Oh, the Places You'll Go!*

Rescue Plan Resource List

Downloadable worksheets, charts, and templates from the Rescue Plan: You can download copies of the Master Schedule Template, the ME Log™, Goal and Step Setting Sheets, and other resources here. http://toomuchonher plate.com/eerp-resource-page/

TooMuchonHerPlate.com: Up-to-date tips, articles and resources for busy women struggling with overload, over-whelm, or overeating. http://TooMuchonHerPlate.com

The How to Put Yourself First 7 Day Blast-off: Seven days (plus some extras) of daily emails, worksheets and short, sweet action challenges designed to help you shift your mindset and start putting yourself first. This program is entirely email-based and is delivered to your inbox daily. You can get the details here: http://toomuchonherplate. com/how-to-put-yourself-first/

The Success Soundtrack™—How to Create More Ease, Joy, Me-time and Success in just 10 Minutes a Day: This audio program which is useful for mindfulness practice and also for carving out me-time consists of short,

10 minute soundtracks designed to be listened to once daily. The program also contains a (longer) bonus audio track focused on helping you identify mindset traps that can hold you back. You can learn more about it here: http://toomuchonherplate.com/successsoundtrack/

Emotional Eating Coaching: The Emotional Eating Rescue Plan for Smart Busy Women is an outgrowth of the personal coaching programs that I run with women worldwide. In those relationships, I work with women to target their specific problems and goals, identify their unique strengths and talents and help them to strategize around roadblocks, crafting their unique path to success. You can learn more about personal coaching and my current group programs at the Too Much on Her Plate website: http://TooMuchonHerPlate.com.

American Psychological Association Psychologist Locator: A useful tool for locating a psychologist in your area: http://locator.apa.org/

Oh the Places You'll Go! by Dr. Seuss: One of my favorite self-help books of all time. "Advice in rhyme for proceeding in life; weathering fear, loneliness, and confusion; and being in charge of your actions." Random House, 1990.

Acknowledgements

One of my mentors from graduate school, Bertram Karon, PhD, has an amazing talent for getting to the heart of psychological healing. In the midst of working with complex clinical situations and clients whose struggles, at first seemed overwhelming, Bert taught me to *simply listen*. Listen and be curious. Listen and try to understand. He taught me to learn something new from every person I work with. So far, I have, and this has been a blessing for which I will be forever grateful.

This book is the outgrowth of more than two decades of work with many wonderful clients. I want to acknowledge these women for their courage and honesty as they worked through some of their most intimidating challenges, and I want to thank them for trusting me to accompany them on the journey. All of you whom I have worked with, whether alluded to in these pages or not, have contributed in some way to what I know about emotional eating and creating peace with food. I have kept your identities confidential, but please know the deep respect I have for you.

To so many colleagues and friends who modeled for me what a happy author looks like, and showed me the value of sharing what we know in a book—thank you. To Carol Frazey and Helene Segura, who pinned me down, knocked my excuses out from under me, and called me out on the "spinach in my teeth,"—you women rock. Maureen Deger, PhD, has run around Lake Padden with me too many times to count and has patiently listened to my plans and ideas and quietly built up my confidence, one lap at a time. I am most appreciative.

Speaking of running, those of you who run know that it can be a metaphor for living. My marathon training partners have inspired me, held me accountable, and taught me to keep stretching (both literally and figuratively!). Thanks to all of the old ATP group, and most especially, Cheri Fiorucci and Arlane Olson. I don't know if you would be reading this if I hadn't done some of the hard work I did with all of you.

My parents Jan and Carol Frisch raised me to know that my efforts pay off. They have always encouraged me to reach for excellence and to say what I know to be true. I am so thankful for you both.

My husband and partner in life, Scott McCreery is due an entire book of acknowledgments. He knows and loves me, listens (and listens), makes space for my dreams, encourages, comforts, and edits my writing like a (talented) mad man. Cameron and Max, you teach me much and make me laugh at the most unexpected times. Thank you for keeping me humble, adding much needed perspective, and underlining for me the value and meaning of words and books. Oh, and your technical consults and the great music you have contributed to my life have helped energize this project immensely.

We are a product of those we are surrounded by and there are so many more wonderful people that have my thanks. I can only hope that the rest of you know who you are. Thank you, thank you.

About the Author

Psychologist, coach, speaker and
consultant, Dr. Melissa McCreery
focuses on the three Os that ambush
successful, high-achieving women—
overeating, overwhelm and *overload.*
She is the founder of TooMuchon-
HerPlate.com, a site dedicated to
helping busy women take control of

overeating and stress *and* add more ease, success and joy to
their health, their work and their lives. Her passion is helping women flourish as they create a lasting peace with eating
and food, take control of their health and stress, and design
lives that are more peaceful, rewarding and satisfying. Dr.
McCreery provides consulting services globally to profes-
sionals and business owners seeking better life solutions.
Her unique approach has been featured in *The Wall Street
Journal, Good Housekeeping, Fitness, Working Mother,* and *Self.*

Melissa earned both her MA and PhD in Clinical Psy-
chology from Michigan State University. A busy woman
herself, she now lives with her husband and youngest son
in the beautiful Pacific Northwest, where she enjoys the
breathtaking trails, island views, and of course, great coffee.
A former PE dropout, she is currently training to run her
tenth marathon.

CPSIA information can be obtained at www.ICGtesting.com
Printed in the USA
LVOW12s1453051213

364045LV00020B/943/P

9 780989 373708